We British

BRITAIN UNDER THE
MORIscope

We British

BRITAIN UNDER THE
MORIscope

Eric Jacobs
&
Robert Worcester

WEIDENFELD AND NICOLSON
London

First published in Great Britain in 1990 by
George Weidenfeld and Nicolson Ltd
91 Clapham High Street, London SW47TA

British Library Cataloguing in Publication Data
is available upon request.

ISBN 0 297 79664 X

Printed and bound in Great Britain by
Butler & Tanner Ltd, Frome and London

Cartoons by Gray Jolliffe

Contents

Preface

This book evolved over a number of years. Eric Jacobs, the journalist, met Bob Worcester, the survey researcher, in the mid-1970s, when the journalist was given an assignment to write up the findings of a MORI poll for the *Sunday Times*.

We were naturally interested in what polls revealed about current British opinion, but polls done for and published in the national press tend to be used as a thermometer to run checks on the nation's temperature. We knew that surveys could be used to probe more deeply, to measure not only current opinions but more profound attitudes and values, to learn something deeper about the state of the nation's soul. We agreed several years ago to see if the data available from a multitude of surveys could be used to provide this insight.

There was, as might be expected, no shortage of material. The trouble was, it didn't match up. Each of several surveys had asked different questions of different groups of people at different times. At first glance, they seemed to cover much the same ground. Close inspection, however, revealed significant mismatches. Fitting the surveys together was like making a table from different woods: teak, oak, walnut, pine.

We then decided we would have to abandon those piles of old research which were so temptingly available and, what's more, totally free. If we were to make an exploration of the British mind that was both coherent and had some claim to originality, we would have to start from scratch. There must be new research, purpose-designed and analysed by the authors.

Our agent, Gillon Aitken, persuaded Christopher Falkus at Weidenfeld's that the project was worth backing. We first developed an

7

outline of the areas we wished to explore. We tested our ideas using qualitative research techniques, focus groups, developing our questions, adding more, and listening to the vernacular of the day. We then devised and pilot-tested the questionnaire and it was administered by over 100 MORI interviewers to some 1,458 people in 145 constituencies throughout Great Britain over a two-week period in February–March 1989. Their answers were then fed into the computers and some 300 pages of tabulations printed out.

There then followed several hectic months of drafting and redrafting as the two authors tried to make the most of the half-million pieces of information the fieldwork had produced. The journalist drafted and the pollster redrafted, passing their ideas back and forth across London – and sometimes the Atlantic – by telephone, letter, courier and fax. Only occasionally did we meet face to face to share our concerns about the anomalies that naturally we uncovered.

We are credited as joint authors of the book which has now emerged. This is true, but by no means the whole truth. A book of this complexity inevitably involves the efforts of many people, including fieldworkers and respondents who endured 40-minute interviews, during which they probably disclosed more about themselves than they had ever done in their lives. We are deeply grateful to our interviewers – and to our interviewees – for their truthfulness, tolerance and patience.

We must also express our special thanks to Michele Corrado and Mary Russell of MORI who gave unstinting help from start to finish. They threw up ideas, checked and double-checked facts and generally kept us on course. We could not have written the book without them. We also want to thank Gray Joliffe for his splendid cartoons and Michelle Iturain-Merino and Ann-Marie Heffernan for their nights and weekends of preparing the charts and graphs. Our text would have been bleak and forbidding indeed without their art to embellish it.

Finally, we offer this book for what it is: a look inside the minds of the British. It was a labour of love for us both, deeply rewarding in helping us – and we hope you, the reader – to understand *We British*.

London,   ERIC JACOBS
March 1990   ROBERT WORCESTER

Introduction

This is a guide to Britain, but with a difference. We did not set out like other explorers to discover the beauties of its landscape or report on its prosperity or describe the quaint customs of its people.

But our aim was at least as ambitious. It was to travel through the nation's mind and bring back a report on what its people thought, felt and valued. For this purpose we didn't have to travel physically at all, like Dr Johnson who toured the Highlands with Boswell by chaise and horseback, or J. B. Priestley who made his English journey by bus and train and sometimes chauffeur-driven limousine. We stayed at home and used the very modern vehicle of an attitude survey to do our exploring for us.

Any writer about the British must always have a problem covering his subject and two, like us, will hardly have an easier task. Britain may be small but its population is large and hugely diverse. How could one person, or two, possibly hope to comprehend its people and report on them accurately and honestly?

This was a problem that worried Daniel Defoe, one of the earliest to try. He was at pains to stress his thoroughness and care. 'Seventeen very large circuits or journeys have been taken thro' diverse parts separately,' he wrote, 'and three general tours over almost the whole English part of the island, in all of which the author has not been wanting to treasure up just remarks upon particular places and things. . . .' All the same, no sooner has he reached page fourteen of his *Tour Through the Whole Island of Great Britain* than Defoe is already relying on hearsay to tell an irresistible story about an Essex farmer who may (or may not) be married to his twenty-fifth wife and the farmer's 35-year-old son who may (or may not) already have had 'about fourteen' wives.

Opinion research keeps us away from the temptation to tell tall tales. We framed the questions and interpreted the answers. But the raw material of our book – the answers of our respondents, served up to us by our fieldworkers – was produced almost entirely at arm's length. Errors in interpretation are possible; fanciful fictions are not.

Touring by poll, we were also able to reach a wider and more representative cross-section of people and delve more deeply into their beliefs and attitudes in a shorter space of time than any pair of explorers could conceivably hope to do on their own, no matter how energetic they might be.

We assembled 369 questions into a questionnaire which was then put before a representative sample of 1,458 adults by our fieldworkers in 251 of the 633 Parliamentary constituencies across England, Scotland and Wales between 2 and 13 March 1989. In their answers, our respondents probably disclosed more about themselves – their habits, thoughts, beliefs, experiences, values – than they had ever disclosed to anybody else in the whole of their lives. The result was some 538,000 different items of information which were tabulated, cross-tabulated and shuffled by our computer under firm instruction to provide us with the subject matter of our book.

Introduction

It is not our intention to reveal the secrets of any individual who answered our questions. What each person told us about themselves remains locked up and will be destroyed, leaving behind only bits of electronic data, unidentified by name and address and accessible only by a serial number which cannot be traced back to any individual.

For it was not about people as individuals that we wanted to learn, fascinating though private lives are. Our aim was to take the pulse of the nation, to work our way into its contemporary mood and at the same time explore its deeper values. We wanted to know how people felt about current issues like the emerging concern over the environment. But we also wanted to know what they thought about questions that do not change, like the existence of God. As a painter fills his canvas with a landscape, we have tried to fill these pages with a portrait of the mental landscape of Britain as it revealed itself to us through the lens of our survey in the first quarter of 1989.

We began, though, in a very traditional way. Like other explorers before us, we listened to what a few selected people had to tell us.

But these were not chance encounters. We did not, like the investigators of Mass Observation before and during the war, try unobtrusively to strike up friendships with the natives by buying them drinks. Our meetings were carefully arranged with groups of eight to ten people who were asked to talk freely about a series of issues we had tentatively identified as subjects for our inquiry. In Woolwich in south-east London our group was young and working-class. In Richmond in Yorkshire, it was middle-aged and middle-class. We did indeed buy them drinks and they repaid us generously with views which helped us to settle the contents of our questionnaire.

It is worth listening for a moment to something of what the people in our groups had to say. For here are the authentic, individual voices of Britain, expressing their own opinions as these were formed by their own experience. They are frank, vivid, and wildly conflicting. (We have put some of their opinions at the head of each chapter.) Having heard them you may well find yourself wondering: can these people all be part of the same nation, products of the same history and culture, the same summers and winters, the same health, welfare and education systems? True, they come from very different parts of the country and points of advantage on the social scale. But to hear them speak they might almost inhabit different worlds. Listen.

On work:
'I have been trying to get a job for ages and I can't get one nowhere. I just can't find one. I won't take a job for £50 or £60 a week, it is just not worth it. I have a wife and two children at home and that is less than what I am getting now.' *Man, Woolwich.*

'I am a word processor operator and senior shorthand typist at the local council. I like my job very much. It is very interesting. I have been there fourteen years. And apart from that I run a home.' *Woman, Richmond.*

On patriotism:
'I think I'm typically British. I don't cook. I eat fish and chips. I go down the Indians.' *Man, Woolwich.*

'When you think of patriotism you think of the royal family and the British bobby and that kind of thing. This is what you think of when you think of England, isn't it?' *Man, Richmond.*

On lifestyles:
'I am common, as opposed to the yuppie type, and my mum is like poverty. But I broke away from them in the last year. In the building that I live in I have got punks, I have drug addicts, I've got friends who have been on the game.' *Man, Woolwich.*

'Sometimes you have to fight to live by the principles you were brought up with. You see these principles being eroded day after day. And then you are called an old fogey.' *Man, Richmond.*

On caring:
'I thought England was supposed to be one of the main countries in the world, isn't it? One of the main centres. All these things like Ethiopia and Cambodia, feed the world and all that lot – we are feeding all those poorer countries and you look at Charing Cross station bridge, and they don't even look after their own. They haven't got their priorities right.' *Man, Woolwich.*

'My daughter has said to me, "Mummy, don't worry ever about when you get old. I shall look after you, and I shall make sure you live in a house next to me in a granny flat and that you are looked after." And I think that is a wonderful thing to say.' *Woman, Richmond.*

On education:
'When I was in prison I spent six months on a course of machine

setting. Lathe work. Now you come out and try and get a job working on a machine. I can make things, like a fraction of a millimetre, but if you get a job now it's all computers. I spent six months on a course for nothing.' *Man, Woolwich*.

'My children were born abroad and I refused point blank to send them to any public school, and we gave up our work and came back home specifically to put them through comprehensive education. And we were thrilled throughout their schooling at Richmond school. And both of them have done very well. They are now PhD students.' *Woman, Richmond*.

On trial marriages:

'I don't think living together to see if marriage is going to work, works. I was living with my girl for about three years and I only got married June last year, and as soon as I got married things sort of changed. And everything else changed. OK, before I got married I used to muck around with a few men and everything was super between us. But it has come to the stage now when I am going to get divorced and get it over and done with.' *Man, Woolwich*.

'I wish I had lived with my husband before I married him. Not that I wouldn't have married him, but I think it is very important because you avoid divorce. My daughter has lived with her boyfriend and she has told me she is very glad she has done it because, she says, "I don't really think he is for me." ' *Woman, Richmond*.

We recorded hours of this and we could have recorded hours more if we had organized more group discussions around the country. But from such 'qualitative' group discussions we would only have brought back more of the same. All those discordant voices, each telling its own story of joy or pain, of misery or satisfaction: which of them could possibly be the authentic voice of Britain? The answer, of course, is that they would all be authentic, which would make the problem of interpreting their significance even harder. This way we could have collected a mountain of stories and opinions, but anecdotes are all we would have collected.

The techniques of 'quantitative' research, however, enabled us to weave all these different voices into something like coherence. They enable us to turn a cacophony into a choir.

By using a uniform questionnaire we were able to find out adult attitudes throughout the country. We were then able to tabulate the answers by demographics – age, sex, employment, class, region – and by other less obvious attitudinal and behavioural categories: political preference, home ownership, newspapers read, whether people belonged to trade unions, how much television they watch and by their socio-political activities, values and attitudes.

Finally, with the help of computers, we could interrogate the huge mass of information we had collected in any way we chose. We could find out, for instance, how many trade union members believe in God; or how many middle-class housewives living in the Midlands are worried about drugs; or whether left-handed Tory supporters prefer pop concerts to classical music – assuming, of course, that there were enough of each type to leave their mark on our survey so as to provide the statistical reliability which would enable us to be confident that their views were genuinely representative of people with their particular characteristics throughout Britain.

But what exactly is this thing called public opinion? For an opinion to become public it has to be expressed and that can be done in all kinds of ways: sometimes by strikes, much more rarely in Britain's placid political scene by riots or insurrections; more peacefully, and far more commonly, in a hundred and one small actions – in conversations in pubs, in meetings, in letters to editors, in radio and television phone-ins, by people attending MPs' or local councillors' surgeries, by articles and advertisements, by speeches delivered to small audiences in clubs or large ones through television or radio. But most objectively and systematically, opinion can be expressed and assessed through the public opinion survey, or poll.

There are many techniques of assessing public opinion by polling methods. There are, first, the simple yes/no questions, like: Europe – in or out? These are usually employed only to establish matters of fact, such as: do you have indoor plumbing? We used this kind of question only occasionally, as when we asked people to say whether or not they were trade union members.

More illuminating are list questions designed to enable respondents to select from a list the behaviour or attitude they most closely identify with. More useful still are 'scale' questions, which explore the extent to which people agree or disagree with a statement and so reveal the depth of their feelings.

When our poll was completed we had our respondents' answers.

But that still left problems of interpretation. Does an answer represent a superficial opinion, or a more deeply felt attitude or, deeper still, a value? Suppose we asked the question, Is marriage dead? Then suppose a number of women responded that it was. It would make a difference if we knew whether those woman were recently widowed or divorced, or whether they had been jilted at the altar, or whether they were 'liberated'.

Or take the questions we asked about people's attitudes to America. Those who responded favourably may have had warm recollections of the war, or they may have American friends, or business dealings there, or perhaps a pleasant holiday fresh in their memories or maybe they just like jazz or Hollywood movies.

There can be all kinds of reasons why people form the opinions they do. But we only know – we only can know – what they tell us. If we tried to track down the roots of every response to our questionnaire we would never have completed our survey. We would have had to lay each respondent down on the psychiatrist's couch. And would we – could we – even then have got to the very heart of their reasons? We doubt it.

If there appear to be anomalies in some of our findings, then we can only tell you – that's right, there are. We came across a number of people whose answers showed that their values were fundamentally socialist, egalitarian and collectivist on every issue on which we asked them to reveal their attitudes, yet who not only voted for Mrs Thatcher in the last general election but plan to vote Conservative at the next election and declared themselves to be 'strong Tories'. How can we account for this? We can't; except to say that people are like that. They are perfectly capable of holding several ideas in their heads at the same time without being put off holding them by the fact that the ideas are totally contradictory. They may not understand the contradiction or they may have some elaborate private explanation which makes the ideas perfectly compatible in their own minds. We do not know because we only know – and only can know – what we were told in response to the questions we asked.

So what did we discover on our journey? How did we find the British?

The answer is complex. Perhaps the best shorthand way of describing Britain's collective mind is to compare it to a lake or a sea. On the surface lies 'opinion', easily whipped up by a sudden storm and just as quick to become calm and flat when the storm dies. Below the surface, like slow-moving currents, lie 'attitudes', which are harder to shift or change. And deeper still are the tides, people's 'values', which possess their own mysterious rhythms and can hardly be moved at all by external forces.

An example of 'opinion' in this sense are voting intentions on the margin – that is, the fluctuating beliefs of the one person in five who is a floating voter and keeps pundits and party leaders guessing right down to the moment the ballot boxes close on election night. People's views about Britain's place in the world are an example of an 'attitude' which, as we discuss below, has been steadily reshaped over a period of twenty years. Belief in God, which a constant 75% of the population has held for at least thirty years, is an example of a 'value'.

Opinion, in the broader sense, is a slippery and unpredictable beast. It can respond very fast to events and to the mood of the moment, but it can also shrug off these shifts in the wind completely. Opinion can embrace a trend and turn it into an attitude or even, in time, a deeper value.

One example of the speed with which opinion can take on a new shape was the environment and pollution, that whole clutch of issues which are now collectively labelled Green. This was a rare case in which we were fortunate enough to see opinion actually form itself in front of our eyes during the period of time we were preparing and writing this book.

As it happened, we had prior evidence from other polling of how the environment was moving up in the public consciousness. In December 1988, only 5% of people rated green issues as among the most important facing the counry. A month later that had risen to 9%, by February 1989 to 14% and by March to 22%. By the time of our own poll, green issues had taken such a hold that 'pollution and the environment' rated third in a list of nineteen issues which we asked our respondents to scale according to the degree of their concern about them. Only law and order and the National Health Service were seen as more important. By then the environment had overtaken every other issue on the established agenda of public concern, from unemployment and the economy to nuclear weapons and Northern Ireland.

The Green bandwagon continued to roll after we had finished our fieldwork. When we asked people how they would vote in a general election tomorrow, support for the Green party registered a bare 1%. By the time of the Euro-election three months later, however, the Greens scored 15% of the actual vote. And by July 1989 green questions had reached the top, with 35% rating them among the issues of greatest concern. And now, in 1990, green concern has subsided again as other issues of inflation, the poll tax and the like have come to the fore.

How had the environment become such a high priority so quickly? Undoubtedly, part of the answer lay with the Prime Minister, Mrs Thatcher. In September 1988 she made a speech revealing a new and apparently deep concern with environmental questions. Suddenly, Mrs Thatcher had turned green and, just as quickly, media interest turned the same colour. All at once, green stories were on every front page and every political party was vying to look greener than the rest. Media interest, as we shall see later, is vital in forming people's attitudes and opinions. So perhaps the combination of Mrs Thatcher and the media was enough to account for the whole phenomenon.

But that was not by any means the whole story. Propaganda and media interest cannot achieve that kind of shift in opinion unless opinion is ready to be shifted. We can see that very clearly if we look at another of Mrs Thatcher's campaigns, which has been even more impassioned and very much longer running and which has also attracted a great deal of media interest and support, yet has been a total failure. This is her campaign to root out socialist ideas from Britain once and for all.

Mrs Thatcher has never made any secret that this was her political mission. And with ten years in power she has not only had plenty of time to preach her gospel but to enact it as well, in particular, by clamping down on the power of the trade unions, privatizing major public utilities and selling off council houses, thereby creating a whole new breed of property owner.

Yet in spite of all this, Mrs Thatcher has failed to win over hearts and minds to her way of thinking. Obstinately, public opinion remains unconvinced. She has failed to make socialism unpopular.

We discovered this by asking our respondents to choose between a series of paired statements, each one of them pitching socialist or collectivist values against Thatcherist or individualist values. The details are in our first chapter. The point to make here is that with each question we found more people favouring left against right.

Opinion, then, can be quickly reshaped and remoulded, but only if the public mind is ripe for it. That is what we witnessed with the rapid development of green concern. We suspect, too, that with the environment we may also have caught an issue taking shape which will turn into a long-term concern, certainly an attitude, and perhaps part of the British value system too, though it is too early to be sure of that. For people's deeper attitudes and values are not easily shifted, as the failure of Mrs Thatcher's anti-socialist crusade so vividly demonstrates.

Attitudes can change over time in other ways. Sometimes they move with the current of events, sometimes they pull against it. We can see trends working in those opposite directions when we look first at British attitudes to the country's place in the world and then at class.

When people were asked twenty years ago which countries were most important to Britain, their answer was clear. One person in five (21%) then thought Europe was most important while one person in three (34%) thought the Commonwealth was, and the same share America. Now, twenty years later, that had changed decisively. When we asked the same question, one person in two (50%) thought Europe was most important while only one person in five (21%) ranked the Commonwealth ahead or America (19%). Britain's entry to the Common Market and the approach of 1992 had taught people that the focus of British interests had changed.

More rapidly, the emergence of Mr Gorbachev in the mid 1980s has tilted the balance of Britain's confidence away from America and towards the Soviet Union. More people still regard the Soviet Union as a greater threat to world peace than America. But not so many held that view in 1989 as three years earlier and some significant groups in the country, like Labour party supporters, actually regarded America as the greater threat.

Whether or not people had interpreted events correctly, there was no doubt that the logic of events was what had caused these shifts of attitude. But the opposite seems to have happened with people's attitudes to class.

By every objective standard of measurement, the people of Britain have been becoming more middle-class and less working-class. Whether you talk about income, education, blue- versus white-collar jobs, home or share ownership or any other indicator of status, the British as a nation have been moving steadily up the class ladder, until now four people in ten are judged, objectively, as middle-class. (For a full description of the research industry's own class system see page 215.) But that is not quite how it appears to the British people themselves.

Attitudes to class are one of the few matters on which we have poll evidence dating back several decades. Exactly forty years before our poll, Gallup asked people whether they were middle-class or working-class. One in two said they were middle-class (53%) and two in five (43%) said they were working-class. When it came to our turn to ask the same question, the answer was very different. More than two people in three now claimed to be working-class (67%) while fewer than one in three (30%) said they were middle-class. Yet, as we have said, by any objective standard all movement had been in the opposite direction. So we were presented with the paradox that, while there are more middle-class people in Britain today than ever before, fewer people than ever are willing to accept the label.

What are we to make of this? Simply that perceptions have changed. People work, so they call themselves working-class. It is no longer a badge of shame to do so. The hierarchy of class has changed in reality, but perceptions of the meaning of the hierarchy have changed even more.

People's perceptions of themselves are all-important in a guide to the national psyche. Nowhere was this more obvious than when we looked at the question of whether Britain could claim to be a Christian nation.

It certainly isn't anything else. No other religions – Jewish or Moslem, for instance – registered more than 1% affiliation in our poll. Whether Christianity is alive and well, it has not been replaced by any other faith.

If you measure Christianity by the number of those who claim to belong to one or other of its denominations, then it is indeed alive and well. Nine people in ten (88%) told us that they considered themselves as belonging to a denomination of the Christian Church. Only one in twenty-five (4%) said they were atheists and the same percentage agnostics.

When we probed deeper into questions of faith and practice,

however, the ground beneath our feet became less firm. A majority
of people believe in God, sin, the soul and heaven. And significant
minorities believe in life after death, the devil and hell. But fewer
than one person in five (17%) regularly attends a place of worship
while a majority (63%) never go or attend only on special occasions
like weddings and funerals.

Probing further still by inquiring into people's moral attitudes
we found little left that resembled the traditional teaching of any
Christian Church. Homosexuality, abortion, having a child or living
together while unmarried, and divorce are all seen to be morally
wrong by fewer than half the population: by four people in ten (40%)
in the case of homosexuality; by only one person in ten (11%) in the
case of divorce.

It isn't that people no longer have moral standards. They do.
But those standards no longer correspond with the teaching of the
Christian Churches. Nor is it that people no longer respect the
Church. As an institution, it is still in good standing. Nor have they
abandoned all Christian beliefs, as we have seen. But it is tempting
to conclude that, while the British like to think of themselves as
Christian, their actual behaviour is guided by codes which are essentially irreligious, by any conventional or traditional definition of
religion. As with class, the perception of how things are is at odds
with the reality.

These are some of the problems and paradoxes we encountered on
our journey. We will not attempt to summarize the whole trip now.
Each of the eighteen chapters which follow is itself a summary and
besides there is no point in spoiling a story by telling the plot when
the reader has hardly begun.

Here, we will only draw attention to one thing: our overwhelming
sense of the British as a people who are deeply conservative (in the
non-political meaning of that word).

This may seem strange. We live in a media-dominated age. It is
from the newspapers and television that people now draw most of
their opinions. Traditional values you might expect to be handed
down the years in a tribe gathered round the cooking pot or by
villagers at the parish pump. But in a society where there is so much
instant news and on the spot judgement you might expect attitudes
to be fickle and fast moving.

But this is not what we found. Opinion does indeed fluctuate rapidly over ephemeral matters like the standing of the political parties. But deeper attitudes and values are far slower to shift. The medium through which opinion is transmitted may have changed out of all recognition, but the traditional message remains remarkably constant.

The failure of the Thatcher years to make any deep impression on attitudes is the most vivid example of this. Thatcherism has left its mark on many things, but it has also left the values of the nation virtually untouched. Socialist/collectivist attitudes are still much more popular than her own capitalist/individualist ones. Nor did we find any sign of that much talked-about species, Thatcher's children, a generation of young people whose attitudes are supposedly in complete harmony with the imperatives of Thatcherite doctrine. The evidence is clear; they just do not exist.

Even the attitudes to the trade unions remains singularly unaffected. A majority of people still think they are controlled by handfuls of militants and extremists, as they thought in the mid-1970s, though there is no longer a majority which thinks they have too much power. Mrs Thatcher's legislation can undoubtedly take much of the credit for that. Yet when the simple statement was put to people, 'Trade unions are essential to protect workers' interests', 73% agreed in October 1975, and 72% agreed in March 1989. In spite of everything that has happened people still, it seems, think the unions are fundamentally a good thing.

It may be that the unions have succeeded in lodging themselves in the public mind as part of the great institutional structure of the nation. Certainly, the traditional institutions are still held in high esteem. The royal family, the armed forces, the Church, the police, the medical profession – they all enjoy undiminished respect. A Victorian returned to life might find it hard to recognize much that was familiar to him in modern Britain. But he would surely be reassured to find that the traditional pillars of the Establishment are still very much in place.

Further evidence of conservatism lies scattered throughout the pages that follow, sometimes in unlikely places. We will cite only one more – the nation's attitude to its possessions. People undoubtedly enjoy the material things that have come their way in recent years, but they are not by any means hooked or hung up on them.

They say they could perfectly well get by without most, even the colour televisions on which they depend so heavily for their information and entertainment. People would be reluctant to give up cars and telephones, and above all the ownership of their own homes, probably because these are perceived as being virtual necessities in today's world. But other things are dispensable: in particular, shares. In the last decade, share ownership has mushroomed so that now one adult in four owns some at least. But almost half the nation (47%) doesn't want them and more than seven people in ten (74%) who already owned shares told us they could do without them.

Another example of the failure of the Thatcher revolution to strike roots? Yes, but it seemed to us there is more to it than that. In the British temperament, it takes a long time to turn an option or a luxury into a habit or a need. That slowness to change is a very British characteristic which, like respect for the Establishment and so much more, we suspect is more durable than Thatcherism and likely to survive intact any alternative creed that may follow it.

I

Political Britain

'SINCE MAGGIE THATCHER HAS BEEN IN, THE RICH HAVE GOT RICHER AND THE POOR HAVE GOT POORER.'

'We are all socialists nowadays,' famously if fatuously declared Edward VII when still Prince of Wales in 1895. Nearly a century later, he might be surprised to learn how much truth still lingers in his wry little joke.

Even more so might Mrs Margaret Thatcher. She has made no secret of her ambition to 'kill socialism' in Britain once and for all. In April 1989, on the verge of ending her tenth year in power, she declared that 'the people have truly moved away from it' – it meaning socialism – although, she conceded, they had perhaps not yet done so 'permanently'.

We would have to put that very differently. We would have to say that the people have hardly moved away from whatever socialist ideals they may have held. In fact they may have moved scarcely at all.

There is nothing simple about political beliefs or behaviour. People have their own values for which they hope to find a political expression. But party programmes are inevitably compromises and they do not easily fit individual consciences, any more than a single suit, however well made, could fit a hundred people. It is often only with great difficulty that people manage to wriggle into the clothes of any political party and even when they have got into their costume they find it uncomfortable to wear. Sometimes, indeed, people seem to get into the wrong suit of clothes entirely. To put it another way, it is by no means uncommon to find people whose voting intentions are in apparently stark contrast with their beliefs. Many strange hybrids lurk in the political jungle. Perhaps the strangest we came across is the person who describes himself or herself as a Conservative voter and even as a 'strong' Tory, yet who thinks all the same that their ideal society would be one of socialist principles, ideals and values.

In politics, we found, volatility and contradiction are the norm. Here are two examples to make the point.

When we conducted our poll, support for the Greens was barely strong enough to show up in significant numbers, we registered them at no more than 1% of the electorate. But three months later at the Euro-elections they secured 15% of the votes cast.

Again, when we asked our sample what they thought was bad about living in Britain today, there was no doubt about the answer. Young and old, north and south, men and women, well-off and poor, were virtually unanimous. The Government and its policies were at the top of almost everybody's list. Yet when we asked which party those same people would vote for at an election tomorrow there was just as little doubt. The Conservatives would have romped home.

Opinion, then, fluctuates rapidly, continuously and often perversely. But underlying values are more solid and harder to shift. The surface evidence of voting intentions may show a high degree of satisfaction with Mrs Thatcher and her creed. But beneath the surface, we discovered, popular attitudes lean genuinely and solidly in favour of an alternative to Thatcherism.

Two things in particular stand out from our findings. One is that the Tories can no longer rely on women's votes to the same extent as in the 1960s and 1970s, when Labour would never have held power if women alone had possessed the right to vote. We found that women now regularly put non-Tory ideals ahead of Tory ones.

The second is that Mrs Thatcher's crusade has not even succeeded in converting all her own supporters to her way of thinking. The 'wet' tendency is still very much alive and well inside the Tory party, no matter how comprehensively 'dry' the party programme may have become over the Thatcher decade.

We asked a series of questions designed to uncover attitudes from several directions. Our questions took the form of a choice between paired statements. We began by putting the choice in textbook political terms, between socialism and capitalism. Then we moved on to pitch the choice between what seemed to us the main thrust of

Thatcherist thinking such as giving priority to wealth creation and economic growth; and the alternatives to those policies such as welfare and 'caring'.

First, and most directly, we asked whether people favoured 'a mainly capitalist society in which private interests and free enterprise are most important', or 'a mainly socialist society in which public interests and a more controlled economy are most important'. The socialist society beat the capitalist by an outright eight points, 47% to 39%: by three points with men but twelve with women; by only two points with those over 55 years but by twelve with those between 15 and 34; by two with home owners but by thirty-one with council tenants; by two with non trade-unionists but by thirty-one among union members.

That overall verdict was clear enough. But perhaps the question was a little too abstract and vague, too ideological to test the pragmatic British. So we moved on to something more concrete – the welfare issue. Did people, we wondered, prefer a society which 'emphasizes the social and collective provision of welfare' to one where 'the individual is encouraged to look after himself'? Again, though, we found that 54% preferred the first alternative and only 40% the second.

This response, too, could have been misleading. It might just have been a piece of empty piety, a generous nod of goodwill towards the neighbours, cheaply made. So we next put something even more concrete to our respondents. We asked whether they were ready to put their own hard-earned money behind their easily-expressed ideals. We found that they were.

Did people, we asked, favour a country with 'a significantly higher tax rate for ordinary taxpayers in order to pay for generous support for the elderly and the poor'? Or were they for one which has 'a significantly lower tax rate for ordinary taxpayers and provides only minimum support for the elderly and the poor'?

The answer was unambiguous and overwhelming – 71% were for higher taxes and generous support and only 15% for lower taxes and minimal support.

There was even stronger approval of higher taxes when we asked if people were willing to pay more towards the National Health Service. Our question was whether there should be a higher tax rate to provide 'a substantially better health service' or a lower one to provide 'only a minimum health service'. A crushing 78% said they wanted higher taxes while only 11% wanted lower.

Notice that we very carefully did not let people get away with saying they would happily soak the rich to pay for everybody else by raising only the highest rates of tax. We specifically focused on the ordinary taxpayer, the 23 million who pay only the standard rate. We found that a vast majority of those ordinary people were willing to see their own taxes rise to pay for social benefits and medical services.

It has to be said that this choice was not easily made. Only from 6% to 14% of our sample declined to make up their minds at all (as with most of our questions). But the great majority who did make up their minds put a lot of agonizing into it. Our field supervisors reported that these 'values' questions provoked the most anguish among our respondents. They hummed and hawed for longer over them than over any other questions they were asked in interviews which lasted close to an hour. But, as we have seen, when they had chewed it over and swallowed their reservations, people did come down overwhelmingly for the higher, and socialistic, tax options.

Their thoughtful hesitation makes their final decision all the more convincing.

But it is one thing to redistribute wealth once it has been made. It is something else altogether to make it. So we moved on to the issue of wealth creation. Here Mrs Thatcher might indeed find comfort. Some sense of her blunt realism about jobs and rewards for hard work has worked its way into the nation's thinking. People do not now want featherbedding in industry and they do want those who work for their living to earn and keep as much as they can for their trouble.

Our poll asked whether people preferred a society 'which emphasizes keeping people in jobs even where this is not very efficient' to one which puts the emphasis on 'increasing efficiency rather than keeping people in jobs'. By five points (47% to 42%) the result was a clear plurality for efficiency over padded payrolls. This result was equally clear among those in full-time employment and equally balanced within a point or two among trade union members and non-members.

Even more clearly, our poll revealed a preference for differential rewards over equality of incomes. We asked whether people should be allowed to 'make and keep as much money as they can' or whether the emphasis should be on 'similar incomes and rewards for everyone': 52% wanted to keep differentials against the 40% who favoured a move towards equality, and the balance was tipped towards inequality, even among working-class people.

There is, however, nothing exclusively Thatcherite in these two results. Differentials, for instance, have long been at the very heart of the pay bargaining campaigns run by the trade unions which back Britain's Labour party. Equal pay all round and permanent jobs for the boys regardless of their economic value have never been part of the British socialist credo.

Other evidence from our poll demonstrates how strong the tilt of the nation's thinking is against the single-minded priority for wealth creation which has been such a powerful feature of the Thatcher Government. It shows people do not want their schools to become specialized only to the needs of employers, by a factor of two to one. They do not want the environment to be sacrificed to the demands of economic growth, by more than six to one. And they most emphatically do want those who care for others to be more highly

27

rewarded than those who create wealth, by nearly seven to one. Three questions brought these attitudes into focus. One asked whether Britain should be a country whose schools gave children 'a wide-ranging education' or only 'the particular skills and attitudes wanted by employers today': 61% preferred the former to the 33% who wanted the latter.

Another question was designed to stake the environment against growth. Should Britain be a country which emphasized 'protection of the environment at the expense of economic growth'? we asked. Or should it be the other way round, 'growth at the expense of the environment'? 75% put the environment first and only 12% growth (incidentally signalling the dramatic rise of the Greens).

Finally, we matched the carers against the wealth creators. Who should get more? Our question was whether a society where the 'creation of wealth is more highly rewarded' was closest to people's ideals or one where 'caring for others' got the higher rewards. The answer to this was more emphatic than any other: 81% were for the carers while only 12% were for the wealth creators.

We do not have a great deal of evidence about how attitudes as measured by these questions have been shifting over time. But what little we do have suggests they have been building against Mrs Thatcher. Several of our questions had been asked in another poll a year earlier. Only two revealed significant movement, and both were in an anti-Thatcherist direction.

Our poll showed that 39% preferred a mainly capitalist society to a mainly socialist one, while a year earlier 4% more registered a preference for capitalism. Similarly, our poll showed that 12% thought wealth creators should be better rewarded than carers. A year before it had been 16%.

Other evidence from our poll helps to show how limited has been the success of Thatcherist thinking. For one thing, it is clear that many Tory supporters possess ideals that are by no means in sympathy with the thrust of Thatcherist policies: 74% of Tory supporters believe that carers should be more highly rewarded than wealth creators; 58% want the schools to give children a wide-ranging education; 68% are ready to pay higher taxes to help the old and the poor; while no fewer than 73% are willing to do the same to boost the health service.

When it comes to economic growth versus the environment, Tory supporters are even more enthusiastic for environmental protection than Labour: 77% of them put the environment before wealth creation while only 72% of Labourites do the same.

Perhaps most alarming for Thatcherism was the attitude of women. In the 1960s and 1970s women were a powerful bedrock of Tory support, but women have since moved decisively against Thatcherist ideals.

More women dislike a capitalist society than do men. More women favour collective welfare above individualism than do men. While more men favour efficiency over job preservation, more women have the opposite priority. Women are much keener on equal rewards than men and keener still that the carers should be more highly rewarded than the wealth creators. Only on the environment and higher taxes to pay for the health service and social benefits do they lag marginally behind men in their anti-Thatcherist leanings.

One final paradox underlines the precariousness of Thatcherism. An astonishing 26% of Tory supporters actually said their ideal society would be a mainly socialist one, including 22% who described themselves as 'strong' Tory.

That paradox, though, should remind us not just of the precariousness of Thatcherism but of all political ideologies, including socialism, in a country where people are free to make up their own minds. Our poll does not prove that Britain is ready to reject Thatcherism for socialism or any other creed. But what it does reveal beyond question is that Mrs Thatcher has not won the hearts and minds of the British people. If Britain could find an alternative political leadership in which it had confidence – and that includes an alternative which called itself Tory – the politics of the nation could soon look very different.

Thatcherist v. Socialist

We can now summarize the complex layers of opinions and values of which Britain's political culture is made up.

First, there is the verdict of the voters at three successive general elections.

The voters made their choice between the alternatives presented to them. Three times they have returned Mrs Thatcher and the Tories

1-1 General Election Results

	1979 %	1983 %	1987 %
Conservative	45	44	43
Labour	38	28	31
Liberal (later Alliance)	14	26	24
Others	3	2	2
Conservative lead	+7	+16	+12
Commons majority	44	144	102

Source: *Times Guide to the House of Commons*, 1987

to power. But does that choice genuinely reflect people's values? Not according to the evidence of our poll.

The poll set Thatcherist values against socialist ones. (We use the word Thatcherist here rather than Thatcherite, to identify the views of our respondents with a set of values rather than with the person of the Prime Minister.) Five pairs of statements contrasting socialist and Thatcherist values, were included in our survey. This was the reaction:

> If we define Thatcherists and socalists as people who endorse at least three of those rival sets of values then 54% of British adults can be called socialists and only 34% Thatcherists.

We can look at this a slightly different way by examining the evidence of another poll, taken a year earlier, in which identical statements were put to respondents who were then asked to say how close Britain was at the time to each set of values and how far that was from the ideal. In every case, the majority thought Britain was too Thatcherist: in making and keeping as much money as they can by some 20%; in increasing efficiency rather than keeping people at work by 18%; in being a mainly capitalist society by 34%; in encouraging the individual to look after himself by 26%; and in being

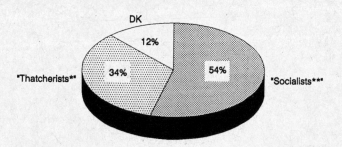

People have different views about the ideal society. . . . which one . . . comes closest to your ideal ?

Thatcherist Values

Socialist Values

society in which the ation of wealth is more hly regarded	12% — 81%	A society in which the caring for others is more highly regarded
society where the individual ncouraged to look after nself	40% — 54%	A society which emphasises the social and collective provision of welfare
nainly capitalist society in ich private interests and free terprise are most important	39% — 47%	A mainly socialist society in which public interests and a more controlled economy are most important
society which emphasises reasing efficiency rather than ping people in jobs	47% — 42%	A society which emphasises keeping people in jobs even where this is not very efficient
ociety which allows people make and keep as much ney as they can	52% — 40%	A society which emphasises similar incomes and rewards for everyone

Thatcherists", 34% of British adults are defined as supporting at least three out of the five statements above

** "Socialists", 54% of British adults, are defined as supporting at least three out of five of the statements above

Source: MORI

31

1-3 Values for the Future of Britain

Q People have different views about the ideal society . . . which one . . . comes closest to your ideal?

Health

A. A country which has a significantly higher tax-rate for ordinary taxpayers and provides a a substantially better health service

B. A country which has a significantly lower tax-rate for ordinary taxpayers and provides only a minimum health service

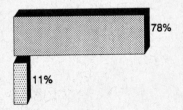

78%

11%

Environment

A. A country which emphasises protection of the environment at the expense of economic growth

B. A country which emphasises economic growth, at the expense of the environment

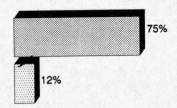

75%

12%

Welfare

A. A country which has a significantly higher tax-rate for ordinary taxpayers in order to pay for generous support for the elderly and poor

B. A country which has a significantly lower tax-rate for ordinary taxpayers and provides only minimum support for the elderly and the poor

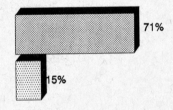

71%

15%

Education

A. A country in which the schools provide the children with a wide-ranging general educatiion

B. A country in which the schools provide children with the particular skills and attitudes wanted by employers today

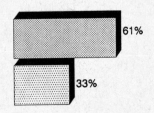

61%

33%

Source: MORI

a society where the creation of wealth is more highly rewarded than caring for others by a massive 59%.

Their five pairs of statements were our core measures for defining socialists and Thatcherists. But five other topical statements were added. They confirm the core measures (see chart 1-3).

So who are the socialists and who are the Thatcherists in our society?

Men are substantially more Thatcherist in their values; women are substantially more socialist; but young and old do not differ significantly in their values. Middle-class people, who are four in ten of the British population, make up over half of the Thatcherists (51%); working-class people, who are six in ten of the population, make up the other half (48%).

A third of socialists come from the middle classes and two-thirds from working-class households. Among the professional and managerial elite, the As – such people as barristers and ordained clergy, captains of industry and editors of national newspapers – six in ten hold socialist values. But lower down the scale, the Bs – among the lieutenants of industry, head teachers and ad agency directors – the proportion falls to four in ten. One in ten Labour supporters (11%) identify with Thatcherist values; but an astonishing quarter (23%) of Conservative supporters identify with socialist values.

Religion makes no difference whatever to political values. Believers and non-believers, active churchgoers and absolute non-attenders, each category is just as likely to hold Thatcherist or socialist ideals. Nor does your star sign make the slightest difference to your political values. If 8% of the adult population was born under Gemini, then so were 8% of socialists and 8% of Thatcherists. Your destiny may be written in the stars, but your politics most certainly are not.

Are there any pointers to the political future in our survey? We believe so. Any political party that seeks to tap Britain's deeper values would be wise to concentrate on collective solutions to our policies: health, the environment, welfare, and education. For it is collective solutions to these problems that people look to as their ideal.

1-4 Who are the Thatcherists/Socialists?

British Public %		Thatcherists (34% = 100%) %	Socialists (54% = 100%) %
100	All		
48	Men	55	44
52	Women	45	56
37	15–34	37	37
29	35–54	29	30
33	55+	34	33
39	ABC1 (middle class)	52	33
31	C2 (skilled working class)	27	34
30	DE (working class)	21	34
36	North (inc Scot)	34	39
25	Midlands (inc Wales)	24	25
39	South	42	36
19	Trade Unionist	13	23
33	Children in household	32	33
22	Shareowner	31	18
38	Conservative	65	23
28	Labour	11	41
7	SLD	6	8
7	SDP	3	9
6	Activists	7	5
14	Consumerists	16	13
16	Environmentalists	17	16
22	Salariat	28	17
13	Routine Non–Manual	16	13
11	Petty Bourgeoisie	16	9
9	Foreman Technicians	11	10
37	Working class	26	44
7	Other	4	8

Source: MORI

2

Green Britain

'I THINK IN BRITAIN WE HAVE BEEN VERY LATE IN
RECOGNIZING ALL THESE THINGS THAT ARE HAPPENING, THE
OZONE LAYER AND EVERYTHING.'

A new, green plasma is pumping through Britain's veins. People are worried about environmental issues of every kind and at every level, from the global to the domestic. They are looking for a strong lead in response to their worries. While they have yet to find one that satisfies them, they are doing what they can to help themselves.

The environment is an issue that we saw taking shape before our own eyes. We have already reported how, in the few months between our poll and the Euro-elections of June 1989, support for the Green party rose from almost nothing to 15%.

We have evidence, too, of the burgeoning of public interest in the months before our poll was taken. As recently as late December 1988, only 5% of people rated a clutch of environmental issues as among the most important facing the country. A month later that figure had risen to 9%. By February it had risen to 14% and by July to 35%. By the end of the year it was back down to 18%.

What triggered this sudden rush of interest? Undoubtedly, Mrs Thatcher's path-breaking speech on the environment to the Royal Society the previous September had something to do with it. She warned that mankind may have 'unwittingly begun a massive experiment with the system of this planet itself'. She described the protection of the environment and the balance of nature as 'one of the great challenges of the late twentieth century'. That speech made the environment news, not least because of its unexpectedness. All at once, green issues were on every newspaper's front page.

2-1 Green Attitudes

Q How strongly do you agree or disagree. . . ?

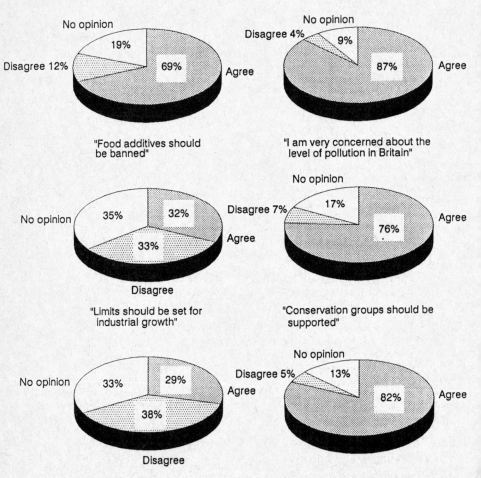

No opinion
19%
Disagree 12%
69% Agree
"Food additives should be banned"

No opinion
Disagree 4%
9%
87% Agree
"I am very concerned about the level of pollution in Britain"

No opinion
35%
32%
33%
Disagree
"Limits should be set for industrial growth"

No opinion
17%
Disagree 7%
76% Agree
Agree
"Conservation groups should be supported"

No opinion
33%
29% Agree
38%
Disagree
"The building of nuclear power stations has been a good thing for Britain

No opinion
Disagree 5%
13%
82% Agree
"The government should ensure that all new cars only run on lead free petrol

NB 'No opinion' includes those who say 'Neither agree nor disagree'

Source: MORI

But the environment does not look like being a one-day wonder or a passing fad: Mrs Thatcher may have helped to kindle a fire, but public opinion appears to have been already dry and combustible, just waiting for a match to ignite it. Evidence of concern is widespread. It cropped up everywhere in our poll, even in places where we were not especially looking for it.

For instance, when we asked people to respond to a long list of statements about every variety of issue – from whether marriage is dead to whether the Common Market is good for Britain – there was a particularly strong response to every question tinged with green: 81% thought that the Government should make sure all new cars run on lead-free petrol; 76% thought conservation groups should be supported; 69% thought food additives should be banned; 63% thought smoking should be banned in public places. But only 29% thought building nuclear power stations had been good for Britain.

When we asked people to respond to the blunt statement, 'I am very concerned about the level of pollution in Britain', no less than 87% agreed and only 4% said they did not.

The depth of public concern emerged even more vividly from one of the most striking of all our findings. This showed that pollution and the environment rate very high indeed among those things that most concern people in Britain now. Only law and order and the health service were seen to be more serious issues.

We asked people to choose which concerned them most in a long list of twenty-four issues, ranging alphabetically from AIDS to unemployment. Law and order rated 52% on the scale of concern and the health service 44%. Neither of those rankings surprised us. In fact we would have been surprised if they had not been highly rated. But the ranking of pollution and the environment next at 39% did surprise us. It came six points ahead of its nearest rival, drugs, and twice as far as that in front of those long-held and deep-rooted British worries, unemployment and inflation. For the environment to have outstripped in our poll those two perennial British concerns was astonishing proof of how quickly and comprehensively the issue had gripped the public's imagination.

Concern about the environment is spread broadly throughout the population. But there are some significant differences between groups which helped us to see how the issue is developing.

First, around 40% of men and women, the young and the middle-

aged all registered keen interest in the issue. Only after 55 years of age does concern fall away, to be replaced by worries over pensions and social security. Still, 35% even of older people put the environment high on their list of worries.

Next, there is a distinct increase in concern the higher up the income scale we look. Among low-earning DEs, only 28% gave it high priority; 37% of better-off C2s did the same. But almost half of high-status ABC1s – 49% – rated it vitally important.

Similarly striking contrasts revealed themselves in the degree of concern shown by supporters of the major parties: 42% of Tory supporters rated the environment high, but only 33% of Labour's.

Add these findings to one we reported in the last chapter – that 75% of people put environmental protection ahead of economic growth, while only 12% give growth priority – and we may be reaching an unexpected but extremely suggestive conclusion.

Could it be that the environment is taking shape as a new variety of consumer issue? A worry that has evolved not only from terrifying

2-2 Who Are The Greens?

General Public

Profile of the
"Deep Greens"

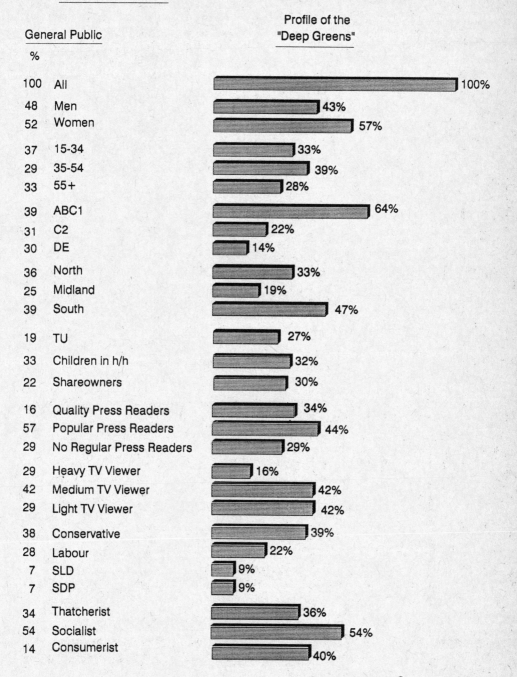

%		
100	All	100%
48	Men	43%
52	Women	57%
37	15-34	33%
29	35-54	39%
33	55+	28%
39	ABC1	64%
31	C2	22%
30	DE	14%
36	North	33%
25	Midland	19%
39	South	47%
19	TU	27%
33	Children in h/h	32%
22	Shareowners	30%
16	Quality Press Readers	34%
57	Popular Press Readers	44%
29	No Regular Press Readers	29%
29	Heavy TV Viewer	16%
42	Medium TV Viewer	42%
29	Light TV Viewer	42%
38	Conservative	39%
28	Labour	22%
7	SLD	9%
7	SDP	9%
34	Thatcherist	36%
54	Socialist	54%
14	Consumerist	40%

Source: MORI

stories about threats to the whole of our planet from the greenhouse effect and the disappearing ozone layer, but also out of the booming prosperity of the 1980s itself? And could it be that those who have done particularly well out of that prosperity are the ones who are especially concerned?

It makes sense to think so. Take a middle-class man or woman with their own home and car, a houseful of labour-saving gadgets and the chance of at least one decent holiday abroad each year. Someone like that is likely to feel they can afford to scan new and broader horizons. What more material possessions do they really want? Few, if any. Far better to take the next instalment of the good life in the form of air purified of car fumes, streets swept clean of litter and rivers and beaches scoured of sewage and industrial waste; not to mention such larger questions as preserving the ozone layer, the rain forests and the whales.

On the other hand someone at the bottom end of the income scale – renting a council house, owning no car, and with perhaps only a colour television among sophisticated consumer goods – can be forgiven for showing less enthusiasm for environmental problems. Once their own domestic environment has improved, maybe that will change; but not before.

Some such perception of the nation's mood would go a long way towards explaining why Mrs Thatcher, against all previous expectations, announced herself to be a Green.

With her acute feel for the political atmosphere, surely aided by the advice of her researchers, she must have sensed how the mood was changing, not least among her own supporters. What's more, seen as new products or further items of consumption, environmental improvements could be made to fit very snugly with Mrs Thatcher's brand of acquisitive Toryism.

That is speculation. What cannot be in doubt is that the environment is now firmly established on the political agenda. Politicians may not have to wear a pure, socialist red in their buttonholes in future. But they will be foolish indeed not to add green to their party colours.

It is certainly on an individual, consumer level that our survey revealed the British to have been most active on the new crop of green issues.

It may be that people would have preferred Government-led public action to protect them. But lacking that they have been doing what they could to protect themselves.

This can be seen at its most dramatic in the response to the scare over the presence of salmonella in eggs and chicken, and listeria in some soft cheeses.

The threat of salmonella poisoning was the big food crisis of 1988. The Health Minister Edwina Currie fanned the flames of panic when she warned that salmonella lurked in almost every place where eggs and chickens were produced. Her statement, uttered calmly enough on television early in December 1988, was dynamite. She said, 'Most of the egg production in this country, sadly, is now infected with salmonella.'

What followed was a classic piece of political melodrama. Consumer confidence plummeted, poultry farmers hovered on the edge of bankruptcy and the Government had to bail the industry out with millions of pounds of emergency cash subsidies. In the end, though, the biggest casualty turned out to be Mrs Currie herself. She was seen to have created the crisis almost single-handed and was obliged to quit her government job and return to the back-benches.

Our survey was conducted in the wake of that crisis, when fears were still fresh in the public mind. We asked, 'Which, if any, of these things have you done in the past two months?' Given up or cut down on eating eggs or chicken? The answer was that 23% had. Given up or cut down on eating soft cheeses? This time the answer was 11%.

The difference between responses to those two questions may not be as large as it looks since chicken and eggs are far more widely eaten than soft cheeses, particularly the brands that were specifically identified as dangerous, like French Brie. It should be said, too, that the cheese warning was issued in more muted terms by the Government's Chief Medical Officer, Sir Donald Acheson, than in the blunt words used by Mrs Currie about eggs.

For almost one in four people to have cut down on such popular foods as eggs and chicken is remarkable. It shows once again how quickly public opinion can respond to messages that reach them loud and clear.

But our survey also showed that messages about the environment delivered less dramatically and in softer tones have been getting through too.

2-3 Green Diet

Q   "Which, if any, of the things on this list have you done in the past two days?"

	1985 %	1989 %	Change ±%
Eaten fresh green vegetables	78	80	+2
Eaten fresh fruit	72	78	+6
Eaten wholemeal bread	51	59	+8
Eaten high fibre or wholemeal cereal	37	47	+10
Had sugar in tea or coffee	54	49	−5
Smoked a cigarette, pipe or cigar	37	34	−3
Drunk a glass of whole milk	29	27	−2
Had fish and chips or a fry up	33	32	−1

Source: MORI

We asked which things from a list people had done in the previous two days. The answers proved a high degree of sensitivity to current doctrines of healthy living: 78% had eaten fresh fruit, 59% wholemeal bread, 80% fresh green vegetables, and 47% high-fibre or wholemeal cereal; and 17% had taken a vitamin pill.

We were able to compare this with a survey done four years earlier and we found that in each case consumption of those foods had increased: fresh fruit was up 6%, wholemeal bread 8%, fresh green vegetables 2% (a small increase, but the base was already high) and high-fibre or wholemeal cereal 10%. Vitamin pill use was up 7% too.

We also found that 6% of people had taken part in a team sport like football, and almost three times as many (17%) in an individual sport or some form of exercise like swimming or jogging. When, in a different part of the survey, we asked a slightly different question we found participation in sports to be much wider than that suggests as 16% had been involved in competitive sport in the previous months, and no less than 42% had done some kind of general exercise or keep fit activity.

Not all the indicators, it's true, pointed in the right direction – 32% had eaten fish and chips or some other kind of fry-up in the previous two days, down by only an insignificant 1% in four years. There was a small if welcome fall in smoking, down 3%; though still one person in three (34%) smokes cigarettes, cigars or pipes. (Tobacco proves the opposite case to the salmonella-in-eggs story. We have seen how quickly people adjusted their eating habits to Mrs Currie's warning. The same rapid response has not happened with tobacco, even though the link between cancer and smoking is one of the most comprehensively established health risks there is and it has been exhaustively publicized for thirty years.)

In another area of health concern, alcohol, the trend was definitely in the wrong direction – upwards: 50% had had some sort of alcoholic drink in the previous two days compared with only 46% four years before. There is no doubt that alcohol is an issue of growing concern, not only on health grounds but for other important reasons too. We shall return to it in a later chapter.

We also found significant differences between the lifestyles of different groups. On virtually every count women have developed healthier consumer habits than men: 6% more women than men eat fresh green vegetables, 9% more fresh fruit, 6% more wholemeal bread, and 8% more high fibre cereal. Ten per cent fewer women smoked than men (29% to 39%); 15% fewer women drank alcohol than men (43% to 58%); 10% more women than men took vitamin pills (22% to 12%); 14% fewer women than men took sugar in their hot drinks (42% to 56%); 10% fewer had had a fry-up (27% to 37%), and 11% fewer had drunk a glass of fattening milk (32% to 23%) – differences which can perhaps be explained by the fact that 10% more women than men (19% to 9%) had also been on a diet.

Besides the sex difference, we also found differences between the age groups. Not surprisingly, older people played less sport and took less exercise than youngsters. But the over 55s also smoked less and drank less (43% of the 35–54 age bracket smoked, for instance, and only 30% of their elders). Older people consistently ate more of the four healthy foods we have identified than their juniors.

Our survey revealed numerous other insights into the way in which people expressed their interest in the environment.

Some activities, like walking in the countryside or by the sea, may seem nothing out of the ordinary; in fact, just a part of normal British behaviour. But put in context with other aspects of behaviour they may take on a rather different look.

We asked people to say which of a list of things they had done in the last year or two: 70% had walked in the country or by the coast, as we have already mentioned. But in addition:

78% said they had either read about or watched television programmes on wildlife, conservation, natural resource or Third World issues.

34% had given money to or raised money for wildlife or conservation charities, an increase of 6% on the year before.

28% had chosen to buy one product rather than another because it was packaged or advertised in what they saw as an environment-friendly way. That showed an even stronger increase on the year before of 9%.

9% subscribed to a magazine dealing with the same wildlife–Third World issues developed in television programmes.

9% more had asked for information from an organisation dealing in those issues.

7% had actually joined such a group.

48%, or almost half the population, had owned a pet.

From other parts of our survey we gleaned further information about people's attitudes. For instance, in the twelve months before our survey was taken, 77% had gone to the trouble of checking the sell-by date on an item of food before buying it, and 42% had checked out food on sale for its additives, artificial colouring, flavouring or preservatives.

Straws in the wind? Or is a pattern emerging out of all these fragments? We believe it is.

First there is what we can call a global concern about the environment. Fed by stories about all kinds of disaster – from the ozone layer, the disappearing rain forests and the whales, to oil slicks in the sea, poison in our water supplies, and disease passed through the food chain until it reaches us in our breakfast egg – people felt a general sense of unease about the health of their world.

This uneasy feeling articulated itself most clearly in our survey in the finding which showed that pollution and the environment rank as high as third in the list of serious concerns, with only crime and the health service ranking higher.

What people may be looking for is decisive action by the authorities. But, finding no adequate response from the politicians to the crisis they perceive, they do what they can to look after themselves. They inform themselves by their reading and viewing. They cut back on their eggs. They shift their eating habits towards foods they are told are better for them. They take more exercise, check the labels on the food they buy, even complain face to face to a shopkeeper (18% said they had done just that in the last year).

There are, however, limits to what such individual actions can achieve and our survey showed how cautious British people are in moving on from mild protest to something stronger. The 18% who complained to a shopkeeper were going further than most. More forceful action was shunned by the overwhelming majority.

Only 9% went so far as to urge someone else to boycott a particular brand of goods or a manufacturer and the same number complained directly to the manufacturer, in person or on the telephone; 6%

2-4 Green Values

Q People have different views about the ideal society. . . . which one . . .
comes closest to your ideal?

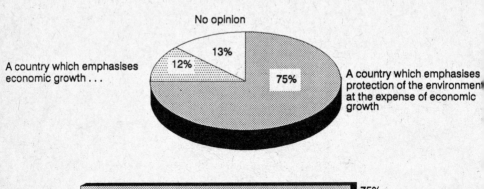

No opinion

13%

12%

A country which emphasises
economic growth . . .

75%

A country which emphasises
protection of the environment
at the expense of economic
growth

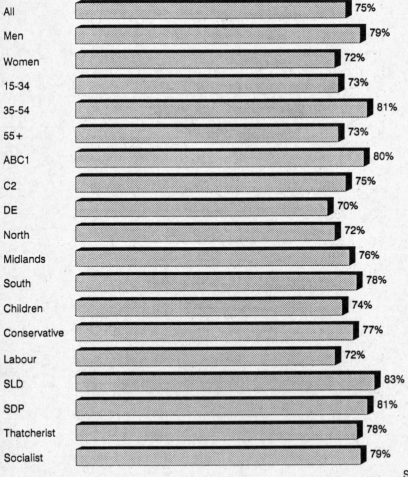

All	75%
Men	79%
Women	72%
15-34	73%
35-54	81%
55+	73%
ABC1	80%
C2	75%
DE	70%
North	72%
Midlands	76%
South	78%
Children	74%
Conservative	77%
Labour	72%
SLD	83%
SDP	81%
Thatcherist	78%
Socialist	79%

Source: MORI

complained verbally to a Citizens Advice Bureau or an independent Ombudsman and another 6% put their complaints to a shop in writing; 5% took legal advice or sued; 3% complained in writing to a CAB or an Ombudsman; 2% or less took part in a demonstration or a boycott, went to a meeting of a consumer group or complained to a Weights and Measures inspector.

Perhaps the most revealing finding about consumer shyness was that while 21% had read the consumer magazine *Which?* in the previous year, a meagre 1% had bothered to join the Consumers' Association which publishes it.

What we are looking at, then, is a huge and complex issue which people fear and worry about endlessly. They would like strong action but they are reluctant to go public and take to the streets or even write a stiff letter to a shopkeeper or a manufacturer. Seeing no alternative they take dozens of small actions to protect their own health interests as best they can.

The environment is an issue we caught while it was still formless and in the process of taking shape. It is evolving fast and what form or forms it will finally take we cannot tell. But there is no doubt that it is now firmly placed on the public agenda for the foreseeable future.

3

British Concerns

'VIOLENCE IS INCREASING. CARING FOR PEOPLE IS
DECREASING, ESPECIALLY OLD PEOPLE. EVERYONE SEEMS TO
LIVE IN THEIR OWN LITTLE WORLD. FAMILIES ARE
FRAGMENTING. I'M A GREAT-GRANDFATHER AND I DON'T
SEE MUCH FUTURE FOR THEM.'

The state of the world does not bother the British much. Most Britons do not lose a great deal of sleep worrying about East–West relations, defence or the value of the pound.

For most people to be interested in a public issue they have to feel a personal stake in it. Great questions of international affairs are for the experts to worry about. The ordinary person will only worry if the effects of an issue strike close to home, or seem likely to.

In public matters the British care about the sort of things that might affect their own lives directly or the lives of people they know and the sort of things they might have some control over: crime, health, jobs, incomes, and homes. These stir their interest because they can be perceived to threaten the lives and the lifestyles of themselves, their families and their friends. More remote issues are seen to be just that – remote and so not very interesting – even if, like questions of war and peace, they could have far more devastating consequences than any others.

This emerged very clearly from the answers to a question in our survey which asked people to tell us which, from a long list of items, concerned them most. We did not make up the list ourselves or pull it out of a conjurer's hat. If we had done that it might very likely have been unbalanced in one way or another, either a worthless, biased selection or an equally worthless reflection of our own prejudices.

Before we compiled it we first listened very carefully to what people had to tell us about their concerns at our informal meetings in the North and South of England. Like ballast in a ship, those meetings helped keep us straight when we compiled the list for this question.

In the last chapter we explored the most striking results to come out of the answers, the high degree of importance people attached to pollution and the environment. Overleaf are the answers in full. Just to make sure we had left nothing important out, we left room for respondents to name any other issue that concerned them which did not appear on our list. But no other issue was raised by a large enough number to be significant. In fact, only three people out of the total sample volunteered other concerns or worries.

These rankings on our scale of concern are clear enough. But they only tell part of the story. The graph shows how the nation as a whole ranks its worries. It does not tell us what groups within the population think. Everyone worries about crime, for instance, but some people worry about it much more than others. Here are some of the most interesting of those sectional differences.

Crime, law and order, violence and vandalism: 52% rated this their top concern. Men and women were at one in saying this, with 52% of both sexes agreeing. But the young are much less worried than their elders. Only 45% of those between 15 and 34 gave it top rating while 56% of older people did. The Midlands was significantly more worried than either the North or the South. While 60% of Midlands people rated it a main concern, only 51% of Southerners and 48% of Northerners did the same. It was markedly more lively an issue with Tory than Labour supporters: 60% of Tory supporters were concerned to only 44% Labour.

The National Health Service and hospitals: this was an issue on which the sexes were widely divided around the national 44% average. More women were concerned than men, 49% to 39%. Fewer young were worried than the old – 40% of 15 to 34s, 47% of 35s and over – no doubt because they had less fear of being ill. The better off were less concerned than the worse; 41% of those who owned their own homes against 50% of council tenants. More married people cared than single, by 48% to 32% – because married people

3-1   Peoples' Concerns

Q Here is a list of things some people have told us concern them. Which would
   say are the four or five that concern you most?

Crime, law and order, violence and vandalism	52%
National Health Service and the hospitals	44%
Pollution and the environment	39%
Drug abuse	33%
Unemployment, factory closures and lack of industry	26%
Education and schools	25%
Inflation and prices	25%
AIDS	24%
Pensions and social security	22%
Race relations, immigration and immigrants	19%
Local government, rate capping and the poll tax	18%
Housing	17%
Privatisation	17%
Nuclear weapons, nuclear war and disarmament	16%
Northern Ireland	16%
Taxation	15%
Morality and permissiveness	9%
Nuclear power and fuels	8%
Common Market	8%
The economy and the economic situation	8%
The trade unions	6%
The value of the pound and the exchange rate	4%
Defence and foreign affairs	3%
Britain's relations with America	2%

Source: MORI

had someone else to care about? And of course, on average, the singles were younger. Many more Labour supporters were concerned than Tory, by 51% to 36%, though most concerned were SDP supporters, at 62%.

Pollution and the environment: see previous chapter.

Drug abuse: concern about drugs, at 33%, was spread widely and evenly throughout the population. The most significant differences were by region and political colour (see also chapter 8). Midlands people rated it more highly than either Southerners or Northerners (37% to 31%); Tories much more than Labour (39% to 29%) with both SLD and SDP supporters trailing behind at 25% each.

Unemployment, factory closures and lack of industry: at 29%, more men were concerned than women, at 24%, around the national rate of 26%. By region, worry clearly reflected experience. At 33% the job-hungry North showed itself more than half again more anxious than the 20% recorded by the labour-short South, while the in-between Midlands stayed in-between at 26%. Labour supporters rated the issue highly at 33% while Tories gave it only 19%.

But perhaps the most interesting group finding under this heading was one that showed no significant statistical difference at all. By class, middle-class people were just as concerned as the working classes; all of them came within a whisker of the national average 26% – which shows that unemployment is no longer of concern only to the cloth-capped working class. Men and women in business suits are just as worried for their own jobs nowadays.

Education and schools: this issue scored 25% on the scale of concern. Slightly more women were worried about it than men, 27% to 23%. ABC1s scored 31%, DEs only 18%. The South and the North were above average in their concern at 28% and 29% and the Midlands stood well below at 19%. More of those with children in their households were, unsurprisingly, concerned, at 39%, than those without, at 18%.

Another interesting statistical non-difference emerged. Equal numbers of the supporters of both the main political parties showed concern about education and schools, both sitting squarely on the national average. In spite of all the recent controversy about teachers' strikes, the core curriculum, and State schools going independent, concern about education does not divide the nation politically; perhaps because few people have higher expectations that one group of politicians can tackle it better than another.

As we go down the list of concerns the interesting differences between groups get fewer, since the number concerned about each issue also shrinks. Such differences as do remain are less surprising. We were not amazed to find that more of the young and single are worried about AIDS than the old and married. Nor were we overwhelmed with excitement to discover that more of the old, the working class (especially DEs) and those not working were more concerned than others about pensions and social security. At this level of interest, rates of concern seem more predictable. Housing, which rated 17% and came twelfth on our list, is a good example. It is of concern to more women than men, to the footloose young than the settled old, to the working class than the middle class, to the crowded South more than the less densely populated North and to Labour supporters more than Tory. Nothing surprising here.

There is another way, though, of looking at this information. Instead of studying each problem to see which groups worry about it most,

study the groups themselves and see what characteristically worries them most as categories within the population. We can do this by examining the responses of different groups to the same issue to see where there was a noticeable contrast.

Here are the most interesting results, beginning with three matching pairs: men and women; young and old; the middle class and the working class.

More men are more concerned about unemployment, race, Northern Ireland, taxation, and trade unions. More women are concerned about hospitals, schools, social benefits, housing, nuclear weapons, and morality and permissiveness.

More young are concerned about unemployment, education, AIDS, housing, nuclear weapons, Northern Ireland, and nuclear power. The old are more concerned about crime, the NHS, pensions, privatization, morality and permissiveness, and the Common Market.

More of the middle-class ABC1s are more concerned about pollution, education, race, privatization, nuclear weapons, morality and permissiveness.

More C2DEs are concerned about inflation and prices, taxation, and the Common Market.

Next we looked at the three regions, the North, the Midlands, and the South. What concerned more people markedly than the others? North: unemployment, the nuclear issue, local government, and rate capping. Midlands: crime, drugs, AIDS, and race. South: the National Health Service, the environment, and housing.

4

The British & the Media

'I REMEMBER GOING TO CHILDREN'S MATINÉES AND SEEING
CRIMES ON THE SCREEN QUITE MERRILY, BUT THAT DIDN'T
MAKE ME GO OUT AND KNOCK OVER OLD LADIES. I THINK
JUST THE FACT THAT TELEVISION IS IN YOUR OWN HOME NOW
DOESN'T REALLY MAKE THAT MUCH DIFFERENCE.'

It was the fashion a few years ago to say that the whole world was becoming one vast global village because everyone everywhere could now live through the same dramas and adventures, real-life or fictional, by flicking the same controls on the same Japanese-made television sets.

To some extent it has happened. Instant global communication is a reality. *Dallas* plays in scores of countries and dozens of languages. Money markets operate in microseconds through 24-hour-day time frames. Drafts of chapters of this book were flashed instantaneously by fax machines between the two authors, one working in London and the other in the West Indies.

But the global village is more potential than real. The world's peoples do not yet have enough interests in common and the British, as we have seen, are not easily roused about what goes on beyond their own shores.

Perhaps one day there will be a true global village. Meanwhile, the British have constructed a village for themselves. It is not the traditional village of thatched roofs and timbers. About the only thing left over from the past is the parish pump, and it comes in the most untraditional shape of a television set.

Today's British village is not a place but a set of communications systems. What binds the British into a community with common concerns and anxieties is what they watch on television and read in their newspapers.

People's viewing and reading do more than anything else to keep them informed and shape their opinions on all the things they feel are important issues of the day. Someone who neither watched television nor looked at a newspaper could hardly claim to take part in the social or political life of the nation, any more than a recluse who never left his cottage for the pub, the post office or the pump could claim to take part in the life of his village.

There is another way in which today's village differs radically from the village of tradition. In the old days a villager could expect to learn many if not most of his attitudes from the people around him: from his family and friends first, then from those stalwarts of the local scene, the vicar and the schoolteacher.

That no longer applies. On very few subjects indeed are the British now likely to be influenced more by family and friends than by what they see on television or read in the newspapers. The Church barely makes its presence felt at all and schoolteachers on only one issue – education.

Politicians do exercise influence. The British actually do listen to them. But their influence on issues rises in much the same proportion as concern over those issues falls.

We can see that clearly if we compare the topic we found concerned the British most with the one that concerned them least.

Crime was the greatest concern. But only one in ten (11%) of the 52% of our respondents who felt it was one of their top four or five concerns rated politicians an important influence on their thinking about it. That put politicians on a par with friends and left them 6% behind family. But it also left them light-years behind newspapers at 57% and television at 65%.

At the other end of the scale, the issue which we found concerned the fewest of the British was their country's relations with America. Here the influence of politicians rated unusually high, at 35%, of the few who did express their concern on this issue. That put politicians ahead of the newspapers in importance – one of only two issues that did. But even this high rating still left politicians well behind television, which scored as an influence with 55% of the people.

We discovered the huge importance of the media when we followed up our inquiry about the issues of greatest concern to British people by asking our respondents which, if any, of the following were important in influencing their thinking about those issues: newspapers, television, friends, family, politicians, teachers, or work.

The answers showed there could be absolutely no doubting the importance of television and newspapers, and especially television. On the vast majority of our twenty-four issues, television was chosen by the greatest number of people as having the greatest influence. Where it wasn't top, television was second or third, dropping as low as third place only on the issues of education, housing, and local government. Newspapers were seen as the most important influence on four issues and on every other issue they also rated either second or third.

Even this does not measure the full extent of the predominance of television and newspapers. Television was rated an important influence by more than 50% of our respondents on twelve issues and newspapers on two. On no single issue, by contrast, were politicians rated an important influence by as many as half our respondents. On only two issues were they rated as important influences by 40% or more. Newspapers dropped below 40% on only five issues and television on only four. On only one issue, taxation, did politicians come squarely within the same bracket of influence, around the 30% mark, as television and newspapers.

The family's highest score was 34% (on education) and on only one issue, housing, was it the most important influence of all. Work's highest rating as an influence was 26% (on taxation) and friends' highest was 23% (on unemployment).

The Church's single significant rating as an influence was 23% (on morality and permissiveness). Teachers, too, made a single significant appearance in our ratings. They came first in importance as an influence, with a 40% rating, on education and schooling. This was the one issue on which another source of influence totally outstripped both media in importance.

Set beside the overwhelming importance of the media, variations of influence between groups within the population look fairly trivial. There are some signs that women are more influenced by television than men (women were more influenced by television than men on six issues and men more than women on only one); while men were somewhat more influenced than women by their work, even rating

DISSATISFACTION WITH THE MEDIA:

what they learned at work the most important influence of all on one issue – taxation.

Similarly, older people listen to politicians slightly more than younger ones. On five issues, the over 55s rated politicians as most influential. The 35–54s did the same on two issues. But those between 15 and 34 never did. Young people, on the other hand, tended unsurprisingly to be more influenced by their families. On two issues they rated family influence top. Their elders did not rate their families that high on even a single issue.

In a sense, of course, all communities must be forms of communications systems. It is both a condition and a definition of their existence and it is just as true of the old village with its parish pump as it is of today's national State bound together by television.

But a community in which print and broadcast media override every other sort of communication as sources of influence as massively as they do in Britain is something new. Family and friends, politicians and teachers, the church and the workplace – they still count for something; but not much when set beside the influence of the great media networks.

Yet it would also be misleading to say that those networks are themselves all-powerful. The networks report what is going on in the political world. So when people say they learn more about issues from television than from politicians, what they may actually be learning from television is what politicians are saying about the issues. Television, then, simply becomes the medium through which politicians transmit their message.

Yet by the way they answered our questions, our respondents showed how highly they themselves rated broadcasting and print above politicians as sources of influence. It may be that people are confused about what is really influencing them. But this can only mean that, if we have not yet reached the point where, in Marshall McLuhan's phrase, 'the medium is the message', we have got very close to it indeed.

So far we have been looking at the influence on people's attitudes of broadcasting and newspapers. Now we take a look at what Britain's reading and viewing habits actually are.

What do people prefer to read and watch? How much time do they spend in front of the box? How satisfied are they with the newspapers and television channels on which they depend for their information and opinions? This is what they told us:

Newspapers. One in six adults in Britain (17%) does not regularly read any daily newspaper and of those who do almost exactly half read the *Mirror* (the *Record* in Scotland) or the *Sun*. Again, only one person in four (26%) does not regularly read any Sunday newspaper and almost exactly half of those who do read either the *News of the World* or the *People*.

Some 16% of the public read the 'quality' national daily newspapers, *The Times* (3%), the *Guardian* (3%), the *Independent* (4%), the *Daily Telegraph* (7%) or the *Financial Times* (2%). Some people, of course, read more than one newspaper. The *Financial Times* has the greatest readership overlap. Roughly one in ten of other quality newspaper readers also regularly read the *Financial Times*.

So who reads what? Quality newspaper readers, we found, tend to be men, 35 to 54 years old, overwhelmingly middle-class (eight out of ten), living in the South of England, light television viewers and Conservative supporters.

Popular newspaper readers form a majority of the British people and more or less reflect the national profile in terms of sex, age and region, though they tend to be more working-class. They also closely reflect the country's political balance, with their voting intentions matching those of the country as a whole.

Non-readers make an altogether less typical group. They tend to be women, 25 to 34 years old, living in the Midlands, divorced and with children in the household.

Television. Five in six people say they watch television every day and only two in a hundred say they never watch at all. Average viewing is about three hours a day. One person in ten watches more than twice the average, but only one in twenty watches for an hour or less.

We followed the television companies in dividing the population into heavy, medium and light viewers.

A typical heavy viewer is a woman, over 55, belonging to the unskilled working class or living on a State pension, widowed or divorced, either not working or working part-time and a regular reader of a popular newspaper, or of no newspaper at all.

A quarter of men (23%) but a third of women (35%) are heavy viewers as are nearly half of the over 55s (46%), nearly half of DEs (47%) and a similar proportion of part-time workers (45%) or those not working at all (43%). Young women, at 32%, are nearly twice as likely to be heavy viewers as young men, at 18%.

A typical light viewer is middle-class, middle-aged, male, working full-time and living in the South of England.

BBC1 and ITV's Channel Three set out to cater for majority tastes and BBC2 and Channel Four for minority tastes. They split their publics pretty evenly. BBC1 and Channel Three each take 34% of the population, BBC2 takes 5% and Channel Four 4%.

But their typical viewers are different sorts of people. BBC1 viewers, for instance, tend to be men, middle-class, light viewers, readers of quality newspapers, and Alliance party voters at the last election. ITV Three viewers tend heavily to be women, DEs, heavy viewers, popular press readers and supporters of Labour.

4-1 Newspaper Readership

British Public %		Quality (16% = 100%)	Popular (57% = 100%)	None (29% = 100%)	Proportion of sub-groups which are quality press readers
100	All	100%	100%	100%	16%
48	Men	54	49	41	18
52	Women	46	51	59	14
37	15–34	33	37	41	14
29	35–54	34	29	27	19
33	55+	33	34	32	16
39	ABC1	81	33	35	33
31	C2	13	34	33	7
30	DE	6	34	32	3
36	North	27	37	38	12
25	Midlands	20	24	29	13
39	South	53	39	33	22
65	Married	62	64	64	16
20	Single	27	22	16	22
15	Widowed/Divorced	11	14	20	12
33	Child in h/h	27	31	37	13
54	Work F/T	53	54	55	16
14	Work P/T	13	14	15	14
26	Not Working	29	27	24	18
29	Heavy TV	10	32	32	6
42	Medium TV	42	43	39	17
29	Light TV	48	25	29	27
38	Conservative	51	40	30	22
28	Labour	17	29	31	10
7	SLD	11	7	7	24
7	SDP	6	6	8	15
10	15–24 Men	10	12	8	16
10	15–24 Women	10	10	10	16

Source: MORI

BBC2 viewers are typically older, middle-class, resident in the Midlands and quality newspaper readers. Channel Four viewers stand out especially for being quality newspaper readers – up-market newspaper readers are three times more likely to watch Channel Four as are popular newspaper readers or people who don't read newspapers regularly. They are also more likely to be socio-political activists, the movers and shakers of British society. (See charts 17 and 18.)

As we have seen, the print and broadcast media are extremely powerful influences on attitudes and opinions.

4-2 ITV Viewing – by Weight of Viewing

British Public %		Heavy (29% = 100%)	Medium (42% = 100%)	Light (29% = 100%)	Proportion of sub-groups which are heavy TV viewers
100	All	100%	100%	100%	29%
48	Men	38	49	55	23
52	Women	62	51	45	35
37	15–34	33	40	39	26
29	35–54	21	30	38	21
33	55+	46	30	23	41
39	ABC1	26	40	53	19
31	C2	28	35	28	27
30	DE	46	25	19	46
36	North	38	38	30	32
25	Midlands	28	24	23	33
39	South	34	38	47	25
65	Married	61	68	63	28
20	Single	16	21	24	24
15	Widowed/Divorced	22	11	13	43
33	Children in h/h	35	30	36	31
54	Work F/t	34	57	71	19
14	Work P/t	22	13	7	45
26	Not Working	37	23	18	43
16	Quality Reader	6	17	27	10
57	Popular Reader	62	60	49	32
29	None	32	27	28	32
38	Conservative	31	38	44	24
28	Labour	38	25	23	40
7	SLD	5	9	8	19
7	SDP	6	8	5	26
10	15–24 Men	6	13	10	18
10	15–24 Women	11	9	10	32

Source: MORI

But how dependent are we on the television sets in our living rooms? And how satisfied are we with what they show us and with our national newspapers?

Nearly everyone has colour television nowadays. Only two people in a hundred say they neither have one nor want one and a further two people say they haven't got one because they can't afford it.

4-3 TV Viewing – by Channel Viewed Most

British Public %		BBC1 %	BBC2 %	ITV %	Channel 4 %	All Equally %
100	All	34	5	34	4	25
48	Men	36	7	30	4	24
52	Women	33	4	37	3	25
37	15–34	36	1	37	3	22
29	35–54	37	5	30	4	24
33	55+	30	9	34	3	28
39	ABC1	44	8	22	5	23
31	C2	32	4	39	2	25
30	DE	24	3	44	3	26
36	North	35	3	38	5	21
25	Midlands	34	8	35	4	25
39	South	35	6	29	2	27
65	Married	36	5	34	3	24
20	Single	35	4	33	4	22
15	Widowed/Divorced	29	6	34	4	30
33	Children in h/h	35	2	36	4	21
29	Heavy TV	24	2	44	3	29
42	Medium TV	35	6	33	3	25
29	Light TV	45	8	23	6	19
16	Quality Reader	50	12	14	9	18
57	Popular Reader	31	4	40	2	23
29	None	34	5	30	4	30
38	Conservative	39	7	31	3	23
28	Labour	28	3	40	5	25
7	SLD	45	6	22	4	24
7	SDP	43	4	29	5	21
6	Activist	48	12	15	14	12

Source: MORI

So the penetration of colour TV is as close to total as we could expect to find in a society where possession of a set is not actually compulsory. But that doesn't mean people are totally mesmerized by television. More members of the viewing public (50%) say they could get by without their set than say they could not (46%). The could-do-withouts and the couldn'ts cut across almost all the characteristics of our sample. Only quality press readers and light viewers by a wide margin say they could do without their daily dose of *Dynasty* or *News at Ten*. Other independent spirits are the socio-political activists, who must be out addressing meetings, and culturalists, who are out at the opera.

A television set by itself is no longer enough for a lot of people. Two-thirds of our sample say they now own a video recorder as well and one in six (18%) say they couldn't do without one. Men are more likely than women (by four to three) to say they are dependent on their VCRs. Those working full time are, by three to two, more likely to be dependent than those not working or working part time. And heavy viewers are twice as dependent as light viewers, no doubt because their VCRs enable them to keep tabs on one channel while they watch another.

All in all, we consume a lot of media in Britain; but some with more satisfaction than others.

People are twice as dissatisfied with the national newspapers as they are with television and fractionally more people are dissatisfied with the Press than are satisfied with it; though the margin is small and filled with an irony. The minority of people who read quality newspapers are much more dissatisfied with the national Press than the majority of people who read popular newspapers. It is reasonable to assume that quality readers are not so dissatisfied with the newspapers they buy themselves. So they must be more dissatisfied with the newspapers they don't buy. Which means that the balance is tipped against the Press as a whole by people who don't actually read what they take exception to!

4-4 Satisfaction With The Media

Q "Now looking at this list of people and organisations which, if any, would you say you are satisfied with in how it is performing its role in society. And which, if any, are you dissatisfied with in how it is performing its role in society?"

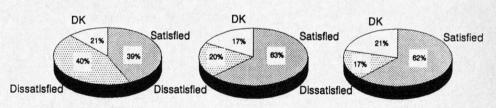

	National Newspapers	The BBC	Independent Television
	Dissatisfied	Dissatisfied	Dissatisfied
All	40%	20%	17%
Men	39%	19%	19%
Women	41%	21%	16%
15-34	41%	18%	14%
35-54	41%	19%	20%
55+	38%	24%	18%
ABC1	46%	20%	22%
C2	37%	20%	16%
DE	35%	21%	12%
Quality	49%	22%	25%
Popular	36%	19%	14%
None	44%	21%	18%
Heavy TV	36%	18%	13%
Medium TV	43%	21%	18%
Light TV	40%	22%	20%
Conservative	36%	24%	19%
Labour	42%	17%	16%
SLD	50%	21%	17%
SDP	47%	18%	21%

Source: MORI

5

Britain & the Establishment

'THE HOSPITALS ARE GOOD. THE DOCTORS AND NURSES AND SCHOOLS ARE GOOD. YOU JUST TAKE EVERYTHING FOR GRANTED, I SUPPOSE.'

Though today great industries and whole communities crumble, dissolve and replace themselves faster than previous generations could possibly imagine, the pillars which have traditionally upheld the structure of British society have managed to survive the turmoil and still stand extraordinarily solid and intact in the public respect.

The British are every bit as satisfied with the great institutions of their nation as we might expect them to have been a century ago. The only difference a Victorian might notice would be the intrusion of two new and strictly twentieth-century institutions into the Establishment – the BBC and independent television.

Otherwise the landscape of social respect would look remarkably familiar. Here the armed forces, there the royal family, and, scattered elsewhere on peaks of prestige, the universities, the Church, schoolteachers, doctors and the police, all still basking in a high degree of public esteem.

Our Victorian might be a little dismayed to find how low Parliament had sunk in the public estimation. But, on closer inspection, he would probably find good reasons to believe that it was not quite as low as it seemed at first sight.

The poor standing of the legal system would probably not surprise him in the least. Have lawyers ever been popular? We have no test of public opinion going back over the centuries to tell us, so we must rely on other evidence; like the 'law's delays' which, you will remember, were one of the discontents that drove Hamlet to contemplate suicide.

We discovered this satisfactory state of affairs – satisfactory for the Establishment at least – by showing our respondents a list of people and organizations and asking them which, if any, 'would you say you are satisfied with in how it is performing its role in society' and with which they were dissatisfied. Chart 5.1 on page 68 shows how they ranked their approval, in descending order of satisfaction. (Net scores were derived by subtracting the dissatisfied from the satisfied, leaving aside those who said they had no opinion.)

On the surface then, everything looks good for the Establishment. The top seven groups each satisfy a majority of the population and the next three at least satisfy a plurality, that is, more people than they dissatisfy. With the exception of politicians and lawyers, they should all be feeling pleased with themselves.

But underneath the surface, there are some surprises. Things are not as calm and bland as they seem. For one thing, support for the Establishment is not always where we might expect to find it. For another, political parties are not necessarily as uniformly unpopular as they look, nor is Parliament; while the sustained denigration of some professions by spokesmen for the Thatcher Government has by no means led to their losing the public's confidence.

We need now to take a closer look at the nature of people's satisfaction and dissatisfaction with our present Establishment.

Politics

The evidence of our list looks unambiguous. The institutions which rank lowest in public satisfaction are all political. The Conservative party, Parliament, the unions, government ministers, the Labour party, the centre parties and the Nationalist parties rated from − 10 to − 42 on the net satisfaction scale. What could send a clearer message of the nation's unhappiness with them to those who rule over us, or aspire to rule, than that?

But it isn't so simple. Take the Nationalist parties, the Scots and Welsh Nationalists. Not surprisingly, they scarcely register a significant presence on the national voting scene at all. Since their supporters must by the nature of their politics be almost entirely

5-1   Political Institutions Come Bottom Of The Poll

Q   Now looking at this list of people and organisations, which, if any, would you
say you are satisfied with in how it is performing its role in society? And
which, if any, are you dissatisfied with in how it is performing its role in
society?

	Satisfied	Dissatisfied	DK	Net
Doctors	75%	13%	12%	+62
Armed Forces	70%	7%	23%	+63
Royal Family	67%	18%	15%	+49
The Police	64%	22%	12%	+42
BBC	63%	20%	17%	+43
ITV	62%	17%	21%	+45
The Universities	53%	12%	35%	+41
The Church	49%	22%	29%	+27
Teachers	48%	30%	22%	+18
Major Companies	43%	23%	34%	+20
Civil Service	39%	29%	32%	+10
National Newspapers	39%	40%	21%	+1
The Legal System	34%	43%	23%	-9
Conservative Party	32%	50%	18%	-18
Parliament	31%	45%	24%	-14
Trade Unions	28%	42%	30%	-14
Government Ministers	26%	47%	27%	-21
Labour Party	24%	52%	24%	-28
Centre Parties	20%	46%	34%	-26
Nationalist Parties	11%	53%	36%	-42

Source: MORI

confined to Scotland and Wales, they notch up a bare 3% support in our nationwide poll. That leaves the majority, the supporters of other parties which look for voters throughout Britain, free to express their dissatisfaction with them, ranging from −39 on our scale among Labour supporters up to −47 among those who back the Tories and the SDP.

What goes for the Nationalists on the small scale goes for the rest of our political institutions on a larger one. It isn't so much the nation that disapproves of them as their political rivals.

Two-thirds of Tory supporters, for instance, are not unhappy with their own party. They rate it satisfactory by a net +50. It is the massive dissatisfaction of the other parties − especially the −82 rating given by Labourites − that brings it down to −18 on the satisfaction scale.

Likewise with the Labour party. Its supporters give it a +33 rating. It is the −54 of Tories added to the −42 of the SLD and the −68 of the SDP which hauls it down to −28 nationally. Exactly the same political bile from their opponents is what brings the centre parties down to −26.

(One in six Tory supporters and one in four Labour were dissatisfied with their own preferred parties − bad news for party managers, especially Labour's, but perhaps not surprising in such a volatile and contentious business as politics.)

The trade unions could try to claim they were in the same boat, sunk low in the waters of public esteem by their political opponents alone. After all, they might argue, Labour supporters actually rated them positively at +8. It is only the Tories' −29, the SDP's −34 and the SLD's −7 that brought them down to a miserable −14 overall.

Unfortunately for the unions, this argument will not dig them out of their unpopularity hole. It wasn't only the politically hostile who gave them a low rating. So did their own members. Only 39% of trade unionists said they were satisfied with their unions against the 42% who said they were not.

Organizations which cannot even command the respect of the members they serve can hardly be surprised if they are not wildly popular with the nation as a whole.

But perhaps an argument that will not wash with the unions will work better with the Government itself and the most important political institution of all – Parliament. Here, too, we see party bias powerfully at work. Government ministers rated fourth from the bottom of our satisfaction scale at − 21. But at least among Tory supporters they rated positively at + 11 (though three in ten (29%) Tories did tell us they were dissatisfied with their own Government's ministers). But it was the concerted dissatisfaction of the other parties – particularly Labour's − 50 rating – which really pulled them into the negative.

It was the same with Parliament. Conservative supporters again showed a fair degree of satisfaction. They gave it + 22 (though in spite of the fact that their own party held a majority of Parliamentary seats, one in three were still dissatisfied). Again, however, it was overwhelmingly the dissatisfaction of the supporters of other parties which brought Parliament down to − 14 on the national scale – right alongside the unions.

If one of the Opposition parties took power, all our political institutions might continue to rate just as low as they do now in the national esteem. But it's a fair bet that the negative ratings for government ministers and for Parliament would come from disgruntled Tories dispossessed of power, instead of dispossessed Labourites, as now.

Our reborn Victorian, ruefully contemplating the decline of Parliament, might now decide to think again. He might then conclude it wasn't so much that Parliament had sunk low, as that party rivalry has become even more intense than it was in his day. The main reason people express dissatisfaction with Parliament in the late 1980s is that the party of their choice has failed to win a majority of seats in it.

A New Establishment?

The Church of England has often been described as the Tory party at prayer. That may be a slander on the Church or an over-estimate of the religious devotion of Conservatives.

But true or false it certainly no longer describes the standing of the Church in Conservative eyes. Our poll revealed a distinct coolness to it among Tory supporters compared to those of other parties. Conservatives gave it a positive rating of only + 26. Only SDP supporters rated it lower, at + 17 on the satisfaction scale. Most satisfied were the SLD at +40. In between came Labour at +33.

Mrs Thatcher's resentment of the Church is well-known. Unlike most Prime Ministers, though, she has dared to justify her political attitudes in terms of morals and beliefs to a gathering of the Church of Scotland. That was brave, but it also seems to have been a failure. Her affection for thrift and self-help – the Victorian values which she espouses – do not go down well with today's churchmen. The distaste of David Jenkins, the Bishop of Durham, is well-known. The opposition of other clergymen may be more discreet but it may also be just as strong.

It is possible that Conservatives have taken their cue from Mrs Thatcher and let the Church slide in their affections as a consequence. But our poll suggests another interesting possibility as well.

Could it be that what we have been used to thinking of as the heartlands of the traditional Establishment, and so natural Tory territory, are increasingly more tuned to Labour's way of thinking?

Look at it like this. Leaving out political organizations, these were the institutions which ranked higher in satisfaction among Tory supporters than Labour: the police, the civil service, the royal family, major companies and the armed forces. (We have left the national newspapers off this list too. Though Tory supporters are more satisfied with them than Labour, that is very probably because they overwhelmingly back Conservative policies.)

Again leaving out political organizations, these were the institutions with which Labour supporters expressed more net satisfaction than Tory: the Church, doctors, teachers, the universities, the BBC and ITV.

It is not surprising to find Tory support for the royal family and the armed forces. But to find Labour people lining up behind the Church, the doctors, and the universities is surely something to make you ponder.

Labour may not yet have taken over as the natural party of the Establishment, but it is certainly making inroads on the traditional Tory patch.

The Professions

Mrs Thatcher's Government set out to challenge and defeat the trade unions and its success in doing so went with the grain of public opinion. Unions are still thought to be essential to protect workers' interests by the same eight people in ten as thought so ten years ago. But when the statement 'trade unions have too much power in Britain today' was first put in 1979, 80% of adults agreed. A decade later, in 1989, when the same question was put, the number who agreed had been cut almost exactly in half, to 41%. Unions are still seen to offer vital protection to workers, but relatively few people still believe they are too powerful. Ironically, one effect of the unions' perceived loss of power has been to swing popular blame for Britain's economic problems towards management. In 1980, only two people in five (42%) blamed bad management more than the unions for those problems. By August 1989, that had risen to three people in five (58%).

Reform of other groups may not, however, be so popular. For our poll shows that some of those the Government has in its sights stand well with the nation. People are satisfied with them as they are and show no sign of wanting change.

The Government's ambition to bring important professions into line with its free-market thinking did not end with the unions. It made little secret of its low opinion of other groups too. Lawyers, doctors, civil servants and teachers were seen to be not much better than dyed-in-the-wool trade unionists, fixed in their ways and as eager as any bunch of Fleet Street printworkers to hang on to their privileges and preserve their exclusivity against all comers.

They were to be given a dose of the same medicine as the unions. Plans were drawn up to change their working environment so that, as far as possible, professionals would have to behave like businessmen, whose entrepreneurial motivation the Government much admires. Schools would choose to become independent from council control and teachers would be paid on their merits. Barristers would no longer have exclusive rights in court – solicitors would be allowed to appear there too. Hospitals, like schools, would be encouraged to opt for independence and GPs to form practices with budgets for health care, which would enable them to cut costs and raise profits. Civil servants could not become businessmen. But their numbers could be reduced and their work hived off into semi-independent institutions outside the comforting embrace of Whitehall.

These were the plans. This time round, though, those who choose to resist will find a great deal more public support behind them than the unions did.

Teachers, for example, still enjoy much public esteem. In spite of their recurrent strikes and the Government's obvious contempt for the unions that represent them, 48% of adults in Britain are satisfied with their performance and only 30% dissatisfied. Among women they rate higher than among men: 50% of women are satisfied with them against 46% of men and somewhat fewer women are dissatisfied (29%) than men (32%). Teachers themselves will be encouraged to know that they rate highest amongst the youngest adults. The 15–34 age group, the ones with the most recent experience of the classroom, expressed a two to one satisfaction level, 54% being satisfied against only 25% dissatisfied.

The one sector of the population which took a consistently low view of teachers were Conservative supporters. On the satisfaction scale Tories rated them a mere +1 against the +35 of Labour supporters, +30 from the SLD and +18 from the SDP.

Teachers may not be able to look for much backing from the Government's supporters. But from the remainder of the population they undoubtedly can.

With civil servants it is the other way round. Though they have never enjoyed a favourable image in the Press or television – where they are persistently portrayed as costly parasites, inept bumblers or wreckers of good government intentions – they score positively with the public. On the satisfaction scale they stand at +10. Overall, more women rate them highly than do men and the old more than the young. But their strongest backing comes from Tory supporters who rate them +16 to Labourites' +7. If the Government tries too strong a hand with its civil servants it could find the biggest backlash coming from its own supporters.

Among the professionals, though, it is doctors who are the great untouchables. Reading through the poll evidence, the problem is not so much to find which group is dissatisfied with them as which group is more satisfied than the others. For they stand consistently high with virtually every category in the population.

Men and women are equally satisfied at 75% each. The 15 to 34 age group is almost as satisfied at 72% but the over 55s are even more so at 79%. The testimony of this age group is all the more persuasive since it uses doctors' services most – a case of familiarity breeding satisfaction, not contempt.

The middle class rated them highly, at 70%. But the working

class – the DEs – rated them even higher at no less than 81%. People who own their own homes showed themselves 72% satisfied, but council tenants were more satisfied still at 82%. There was hardly any difference between party supporters, except on which of them were most satisfied: 73% of Tories were, 78% Labour, 74% SLD and 72% SDP.

If doctors choose to dig in for a long fight they are likely to have support from all corners. The Government will then have to contend with its own supporters as much as with every other party's.

The very opposite is the case with reform of the legal system. If the Government chooses to persist with its reform plans there, it will find as much popular backing as it could possibly want.

With the doctors we found groups vying to demonstrate their satisfaction. With the legal system it was the other way around. Dissatisfaction was too widespread and uniform for us to discover major and genuinely significant differences between groups. The 35 to 54-year-olds were more disenchanted than those older and younger and so were C2s. People who were married, or had children, or were in work or were readers of popular newspapers were less satisfied than those who were their opposites.

But these were straws in the wind. The important fact is that at − 10 on the satisfaction scale the legal system was the only strictly

non-political institution on our list to receive a negative rating. Clearly, the 'law's delays' – not to mention its risks and costs – rankle as much now as in Shakespeare's time and if the Government takes an axe to the system nobody will grieve, except maybe the legal profession itself.

National Newspapers

Here is what Sherlock Holmes might have called a curious case. Why do people apparently disapprove of something with which they so obviously like to indulge themselves?

National newspapers just slipped into a negative rating in our survey at −1 on the satisfaction scale. But more then 70% of the adult population read at least one national newspaper not less than two or three times in the average week. As we have seen, they rely on them second only to television for their information and opinions on virtually every public issue. So why the poor opinion of them? It isn't as if people couldn't avoid the newspapers if they wanted. Unlike the police or the legal system, newspapers are an option people can choose to have or do without as they wish.

The answer lies in a mixture of sex, political, and class differences. Overall, men rate newspapers positively, while women don't. Men give them +2 on the satisfaction scale, women −4. That alone is enough to tip the balance of satisfaction against the newspapers. It may be that the treatment of women in popular newspapers – page three girls and all – turns more women off than it turns men on.

Class differences have a part to play too. Middle-class respondents, who tend to be quality newspaper readers, gave the national Press a heavy disapproval rating with a negative −12 satisfaction score while working-class readers rated the newspapers positively at +6. Readers of quality newspapers, whether middle-class or not, gave the national Press thumbs down − −16 on the scale − while popular newspaper readers approved with a +9. This bears out what we found in the last chapter, that the disapproval of quality newspaper readers for the popular newspapers they don't read is enough to tilt the balance of opinion against the national Press as a whole.

Political differences have the same effect. Tory supporters gave the national newspapers a rating of +6, Labour a negative −3. Add to that the combined disapproval of centre party supporters and 'don't knows' and the overall rating again slips to -1. The strongly pro-Conservative bias of the national Press explains this particular form of anti-newspaper prejudice plainly enough.

The Royal Family

In spite of the heavy exposure of their faults and foibles on television and in the newspapers, the royal family still stands high in public favour. Only doctors and the armed forces are seen to be performing their social roles better.

Approval rates, though, vary widely. Women rate the royals significantly higher than men, $+53$ on our scale against men's $+43$. Older people are much more satisfied than younger. The over 55s give $+60$; the 35 to 54-year-olds manage $+55$, while the 15–34 age group could only muster $+33$. Single people, mainly younger, are less enthusiastic for royalty. On our scale they give only $+31$ approval while married people give $+50$ and the older group, including widows and divorcees, $+66$.

Differences, though not major ones, are also visible in class support. ABC1s are $+52$ satisfied while DEs rate the royals at $+48$. The royal family is especially popular in the Midlands. There it scores $+58$ on the scale while it can raise only $+47$ in the South and $+43$ in the North.

When it comes to politics, SLD supporters turned out to be the most eager royalists. They rate the royals at $+66$ on the scale. Tory supporters come next at $+58$, the 'don't knows' at $+57$, SDP $+53$ and Labour supporters a relatively meagre $+38$.

But if the royal family thinks it can improve its standing among the young, the single, and Labour supporters by shedding its image as the cast of some vast, unending television soap opera it should think again. Heavy TV viewers are among its most loyal fans. The more television they watch, the more people approve of the royals. Those who watch the most give the royal family a $+53$ rating on our satisfaction scale. Medium viewers give it $+49$, and light viewers only $+44$.

Whatever else we may say about the royal family we have to agree one thing. It plays well on the box.

6

Religious Britain

'BRITAIN USED TO BE RELIGIOUS, BUT IT ISN'T NO MORE.
BEFORE, EVERYONE USED TO GO TO CHURCH AND IT WAS
THE IN THING. NOW IT IS CHANGED AND NO ONE GOES NO
MORE AND WHEN THEY DO GO THEY ARE CALLED BIBLE-
BASHERS. THEY ARE OUTCASTS. MOST PEOPLE SEE THEM AS
THAT.'

Christianity has played a vital part in Britain's story. For centuries it helped to decide who were the nation's enemies and allies and determined who could sit in Parliament. English literature speaks with a Christian voice and Christian churches and cathedrals are one of the great glories of the landscape. Still today, no Catholic King or Queen can reign over the nation and schools must start the day with an act of worship.

But can Britain still truly be called a Christian nation? One thing at least we can clear up right away. It certainly isn't anything else. There is much talk of Britain having become a multi-faith society. But our survey threw up little evidence of this. Only about 1% of our respondents was Jewish and another 1% Moslem. Other non-Christian faiths registered only a further 1% between them. When we talk about how religious the British may be we still overwhelmingly mean, how Christian?

The answer to that question, we discovered, varies according to what we mean by it. If we mean, do people wish to be identified with one or another denomination of the Christian Church, then the answer is an overwhelming 'yes'. If we mean, do they subscribe to the central beliefs of the Christian faith, then the answer will be much less confident, but it will still be a hesitant 'yes'.

But if we mean, do they follow through their identification with a church and their attachment to Christian beliefs by regular or frequent church-going, then the answer must be an emphatic 'no'.

It seems natural for the British to think of themselves as Christians. But whether religion plays an important part in their daily lives is altogether more doubtful.

We began by asking our respondents what they considered to be their religious denomination. Few people said they did not belong to any church whatever. Only 4% said they were atheists, with no belief in God at all. Another 4% said they were agnostic, the 'don't knows' of religious belief. But as many as 88% claimed to belong to one Christian denomination or another.

One in eight, 13%, said they were Roman Catholics, which adds up to some 5.5 million adults. Two-thirds, 65%, said they belonged to their national church, the Churches of England, Scotland, Wales or Ireland, numbering more than 27 million people. One in fourteen, 7%, said they belonged to one of the Free or non-conformist churches, nearly three million. And one in twenty-five, 4%, said they were affiliated to other Christian churches, around 1.5 million.

When it came to matching association with a church to attendance at it, however, the picture looked very different. Englishmen may say they belong to the Church of England, and Scots to the Church of Scotland. The people as a whole may still, as we saw in the last chapter, have a great deal of respect for their church. But taken together these do not seem to make a sufficient motive for actual church attendance. As a nation, the British are at best indifferent worshippers.

Only 17% of people claim to go to a place of worship regularly; 22% go occasionally; 43% go on special occasions like weddings and funerals; and 18% never go at all. Women are better attenders than men. Only 16% of women never go against 20% of men. And 20% of women claim to go regularly, meaning at least once a fortnight, while only 13% of men do the same.

The young are less eager attenders than the old: 19% of 15 to 34-year-olds never go against 16% of the over-55s. Almost one in four of this older age group (23%) claim to be regular worshippers, nearly double the 12% of the younger group who make the same claim.

The key finding here is that fewer than one person in five (17%)

is a regular church-goer. Typical attenders are 20% more likely to be women than men, a quarter more likely to be over 55 than under, two times more likely to be middle-class than working-class but hardly more likely to vote Tory than Labour or one of the centre parties – further confirmation that the Church can no longer be described as the Tory party at prayer.

Britain, we conclude, may think of itself as a Christian country. But that claim is not supported by the willingness of its people to undertake public acts of worship in the church to which they claim to belong. The Church may still command respect as an institution but its real influence over people's lives, as we saw when we examined what influences shaped the nation's attitudes, is very small indeed, playing a significant part only in views about morality and permissiveness, and even then only a minor part.

6-1 We Believe

Q   Which, if any, of the things I'm going to read out do you believe in?

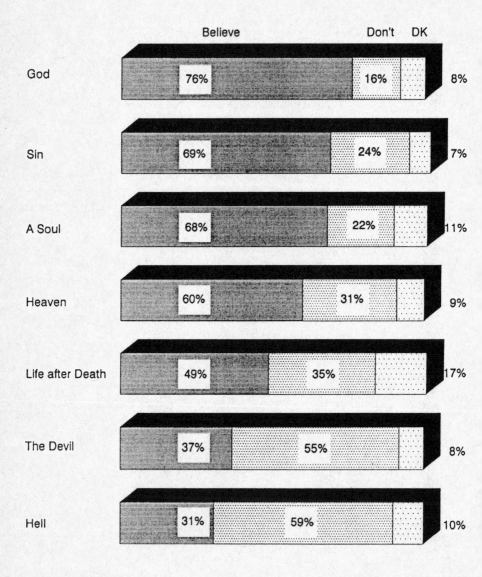

	Believe	Don't	DK
God	76%	16%	8%
Sin	69%	24%	7%
A Soul	68%	22%	11%
Heaven	60%	31%	9%
Life after Death	49%	35%	17%
The Devil	37%	55%	8%
Hell	31%	59%	10%

Source: MORI

Measured by their church-going habits, the British are not a very religious people. But measured by their belief in some of the central tenets of Christianity their faith looks somewhat deeper.

A majority of people believe in the existence of God, sin, the soul, and heaven while significant minorities believe in life after death, the devil and hell.

The figures for each are shown in the chart opposite.

There is evidently some confusion here. More people believe in heaven than in life after death, even though in the Christian faith the two are inseparable. Again, 16% of our respondents said they did not believe in God, though only 4% called themselves atheists.

It is tempting to be cynical about this and say that people wear their religion as lightly as costume jewellery, picking out only those pieces which they think suit them. They are more willing to believe in attractive notions like God, the soul and heaven than they are in more dismal propositions like the devil and hell. Their readiness to believe in sin can perhaps be seen as a generalized belief in the awfulness of man, of which there is plenty of evidence in today's world, rather than in sin as a specifically Christian view of wrong-doing.

Looked at like this, religious belief comes to seem like a variety of consumer choice. You drop the brands you like the look of into your supermarket trolley and ignore the ones you don't.

But this would be going too far. There are limits to what can be divined by an opinion poll. To explore the true depths of people's religion – their deepest beliefs about life and death and the hereafter – has to be beyond the scope of our inquiry.

What we can say with confidence is that women are more prone to believe than men and the old more than the young.

Men and women are equally ready to identify themselves with a Christian denomination. But women, as we have already seen, are much more likely to go to church than men and they hold much stronger positive beliefs than men do:

84% of women believe in God, but only 67% of men
9% of women say they do not believe in God, but nearly twice that many men (16%) say the same

72% of women believe in sin and 66% of men
27% of men do not believe in sin and 21% of women

76% of women believe in the soul and 58% of men
14% of women do not believe in the soul, but 30% of men

69% of women believe in heaven and 50% of men
22% of women do not believe in heaven, to 40% of men

57% of women believe in life after death and 39% of men
25% of women do not believe in life after death, to 45% of men

42% of women believe in the devil, to 32% of men
50% of women do not believe in the devil and 60% of men

35% of women believe in hell and 27% of men
55% of women do not believe in hell to 64% of men

Belief divides the old and the young with the same sort of consistency as it does women and men. Only 67% of those between 15 and 34 believe in God, for instance, while 87% of those over 55 believe in Him. Only 55% of the younger age group believe in heaven while 65% of the oldest do. Hell is the only one in our list of beliefs where there is no significant difference between the age groups, which all come within one percentage point of the average.

We are relieved to report that God, at least, is not a political issue. The major parties are almost at one on Him, if on little else: 78% of Tory supporters believe in God and 77% of Labour. SDP supporters show a slight tendency to scepticism: only 72% of them are convinced.

They also show an above-average readiness to believe in hell: 35% of them do, to only 31% of Labour and Tory supporters.

Conservatives, on the other hand, outdo Labour in their belief in sin and in life after death: 73% believe in sin, more than the supporters of any other party and 7% more than Labour backers. Some 49% of Conservative supporters believe in life after death and only 44% of Labour, though both SLD (60%) and SDP (54%) are even more convinced.

Labour supporters' reluctance to believe in life after death sits somewhat oddly with another belief – their enthusiasm for heaven: 64% of Labour supporters believe in heaven, four per cent more than the supporters of any other party, but only 44% believe in life after

death; which means that 20% more Labour supporters believe in heaven than believe there is life after death.

Could it be that Socialists expect to create heaven on earth, to build Jerusalem here, in Blake's words, 'on England's green and pleasant land'? Utopia has always been part of the socialist dream, after all, and it has always been looked for on earth, not elsewhere. If that is what Labour supporters mean by heaven it would certainly fill the statistical gap that yawns between those who believe in life after death and those who only believe in heaven.

Labour supporters, though, are markedly less likely to go to church than supporters of other parties: 22% say they never go and only 13% attend regularly, compared with 14% and 18% of Tories. The most frequent church-goers are SLD supporters, 26% of whom describe themselves as regular attenders.

In the last chapter we noted how Tory supporters seemed to be losing sympathy with the Church of England. That, however, does not mean they do not still claim identification with their national Church: 70% of Tories gave that as their religious denomination to only 61% of Labour supporters; 12% of Roman Catholics support the Tories. But Catholics show a marked preference for Labour – 16%.

We took a calculated gamble when we added two more items to the list of beliefs on which we asked our respondents to pass judgement. They were astrology and public opinion polls.

For it would have made us feel extremely foolish if it turned out that nobody believed in opinion polls, the very technique on which our book is based. That would have faced us with the choice of either not publishing our book or suppressing that particular result, which is something no self-respecting pollster could allow. To have admitted in these pages that people did not believe in the technique we have used to write them would be rather like printing it with evaporating ink!

Fortunately, we can come clean. Our gamble paid off. A majority of people say they do believe in opinion polls. And a great many more believe in them than do in astrology: 56% of the population believe in opinion polls, 37% in astrology.

Women, we are sorry to report, believe less strongly than men in opinion polls and more strongly in astrology. In fact, almost as many women believe in astrology as disbelieve: 44% against 46%. Men take a more sceptical view. Only 30% of them believe in astrology while a robust 65% do not. Among women, 54% say they believe in opinion polls against 59% of men.

Like God, belief in astrology and opinion polls did not divide the supporters of the major parties. Labour and Tory supporters were both bang on the national average at 37% in their belief in astrology. Likewise 58% of both Tory and Labour supporters believed in opinion polls, against a national average of 56%.

Dr David Owen may, though, be surprised to learn that when it comes to astrology his supporters are significantly more prone to accept its claims than their erstwhile Alliance partners in the SLD: 39% of SDP supporters believe in astrology while only 28% of SLD do likewise.

Finally, among political categories, we couldn't help noticing that our old friends the 'don't knows' showed a tendency to be especially sceptical about opinion polls. Only 48% of the political 'don't knows' believed in opinion polls compared with the national average of 56%. But at least the 'don't knows' have the virtue of consistency. They really do stay true to form. They were also the group most prone to say they 'don't know' when asked if they believed in opinion polls.

Truly, there is no convincing some people.

7

Moral Britain

'I WAS LIVING WITH MY WIFE FOR FOUR YEARS AND WE HAD
TWO CHILDREN. WE ONLY GOT MARRIED LAST YEAR. I DON'T
THINK THERE IS NOTHING WRONG WITH THAT.'

British people may still like to call themselves Christian though, as
we saw in the last chapter, their beliefs are shaky and their enthusiasm
for worship slight. But when it comes to morals they have removed
themselves even further from conventional Christianity than we have
yet suggested. The British today, we have to report, are scarcely in
touch with anything recognizable as a traditional Christian moral
agenda.

It isn't that they have abandoned all moral beliefs; far from it.
They have strong views about right and wrong. But their priorities –
those actions they are most likely to think wrong and those they are
least likely to think so – would no longer come close to matching
those of any established Christian church.

Particularly in matters of sexual behaviour, today's Britons take
an altogether more relaxed view than traditional religion would have
them do. Adultery is the only sexual sin which the majority condemn,
and a majority of men do not even condemn that.

If we were seeking to nominate a natural moral leader for the
nation it is, strange though it may seem, Mrs Mary Whitehouse who
would emerge as our strongest candidate. Her tireless campaign to
clean up our television screens puts her much more in tune with the
British people than the prescriptions for actual moral behaviour that
we might expect to hear from the Archbishops of Canterbury or
York.

For people, we found, are far more likely to be outraged by seeing

85

something violent or sexually explicit on their television screens than they are by sexual behaviour that offends conventional religious belief. Many more people rate violence on television seriously than do abortion and many more deplore full-frontal male nudity than do divorce.

If there is still something puritanical left in British attitudes, it is about what is seen in public rather than whatever people may want to get up to in their personal lives.

Some may see in our findings a moral world turned upside down. They will think it exceedingly strange and deeply alarming that the nation should be more worried about what happens on their screens than what goes on in their bedrooms.

Others will see today's attitudes as a welcome adjustment to the realities of the modern world and infinitely preferable to those times when what happened in the bedroom was almost the only moral issue that could be counted on to raise a lather of anger and indignation.

Whatever your personal views, we have no doubt you will find

something in our results that surprises and maybe offends you. Why, for instance, should euthanasia and capital punishment rate so far below experiments on animals as matters of moral disapproval? Or soft porn magazines so far above divorce? The British live in a new moral universe which will seem repugnant to many and strange to others. But it is one with which everyone will have to come to terms, including the Churches.

We deliberately compiled our list of moral issues as a mixture of old and new problems – drug-taking, for instance, alongside adultery – in order to test attitudes to both against each other. We left off most issues of crime and violence because it was unlikely that people would do anything other than mark them down as wrong, and also because we deal with them elsewhere.

Hard drugs came at the top of our list and soft drugs only a little lower down. Drugs have clearly emerged as a major social worry. So has alcohol. We will return to them in the next chapter. Together they are important enough to deserve discussion on their own.

Soccer hooliganism came second, way above other issues that might be thought of more widespread importance to the great majority of people (86%) who never go near a game of football. It is all the more remarkable when we remember that our poll was taken before the appalling tragedy at the Hillsborough stadium in Sheffield, which again raised the whole question of behaviour at football matches to the level of a major and highly fraught national issue. What is surprising is not that people thought hooliganism wrong but that they should have rated it so high on the scale of immorality at a time when it was not on the front pages. Here, we will only note its importance. We shall return to it later, in our chapter on crime.

People's abhorrence of experiments on both animals and human embryos is also remarkable. Much of the discussion on both issues has accepted that there must be safeguards but has assumed popular acceptance of the principle that there should be controlled experiments on living beings. Our survey shows clearly that half the population thinks any form of experiment morally wrong.

We found particularly fascinating the way people thought of representations of sex and violence as immoral compared to the immorality they attached to actual items of sexual behaviour.

Our list included five items about representation and six about behaviour.

The five which were about representation – television violence, cinema pornography, soft porn magazines, strip shows, and page three girls – ranked between 4 and 17 on our list, or from 53% who thought them wrong down to 21%.

The six which were about actual sexual behaviour – homosexuality, abortion, having a child outside marriage, setting up sperm banks, unmarrieds living together, and divorce – ranked from 9 to 20 on our list, or in percentage terms from 40% to 11%.

This reveals a high degree of moral acceptance of the reality of our world, in which more and more people live together without benefit of marriage and do not think it wrong to have children without a wedding licence either. One in eight children are now being brought up in families with only one parent and the number of such families now exceeds one million, while almost four in ten marriages, according to the Office of Population Censuses and Surveys, are now heading for the break-up of divorce.

When, on top of those facts of current British life, we find that only around one in four people think it wrong to have children outside wedlock, only around one in eight think it wrong for couples to live together unmarried and a mere one in ten think it wrong for married couples to get divorced, we might ask whether the institution of marriage is now regarded as having any importance at all.

The answer to that question is that people do indeed think marriage remains important. When we put the blunt statement 'marriage is dead' to our respondents, their attitudes were clear enough. Only one person in twenty (5%) agreed strongly while another one in twenty (5%) tended to agree. But eight out of ten took the opposite view, with one person in four (25%) tending to disagree and more than half (53%) disagreeing strongly. Marriage, it appears, is still much respected, but the moral stigma which once attached to what used to be called irregular liaisons – creating the wretched figures of 'the mistress', 'the bastard' and 'the unmarried mother' – may be on the point of vanishing completely.

7-1   British Morality

Q Here is a list of issues some people might think are immoral or morally
wrong. Which of them, if any, do you personally think are morally wrong?

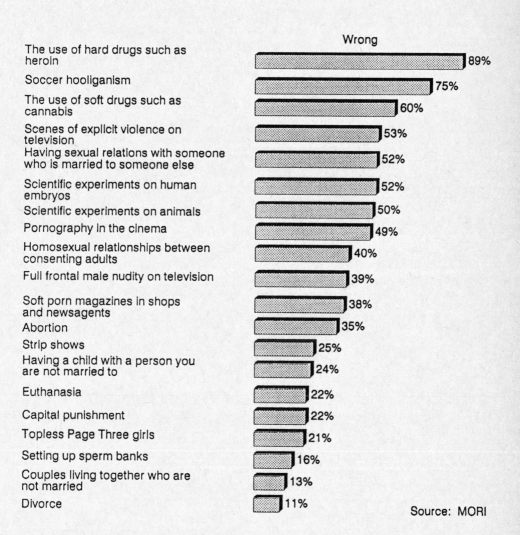

	Wrong
The use of hard drugs such as heroin	89%
Soccer hooliganism	75%
The use of soft drugs such as cannabis	60%
Scenes of explicit violence on television	53%
Having sexual relations with someone who is married to someone else	52%
Scientific experiments on human embryos	52%
Scientific experiments on animals	50%
Pornography in the cinema	49%
Homosexual relationships between consenting adults	40%
Full frontal male nudity on television	39%
Soft porn magazines in shops and newsagents	38%
Abortion	35%
Strip shows	25%
Having a child with a person you are not married to	24%
Euthanasia	22%
Capital punishment	22%
Topless Page Three girls	21%
Setting up sperm banks	16%
Couples living together who are not married	13%
Divorce	11%

Source: MORI

One other point is worth noting here. In every question of representation on television, cinema or magazines, women were much more hostile than men:

61% of women rated explicit violence on television immoral to 45% of men;

54% of women rated cinema pornography immoral to 43% of men;

43% of women rated male nudity on television immoral to 34% of men;

46% of women thought soft porn magazines immoral to 29% of men;

29% of women thought strip shows immoral to 21% of men;

24% of women thought page three girls immoral to 17% of men.

7-2   Moralists and Free-Thinkers

				Proportion of sub-groups which are:	
British Public %		Moralists (9% = 100%)	Free-Thinkers (7% = 100%)	Moralists	Free-Thinkers
100	All	100%	100%	9%	7%
48	Men	39	63	7	9
52	Women	61	37	10	5
37	15-34	14	47	3	9
29	35-54	24	35	7	8
33	55+	62	18	17	4
39	ABC1	40	37	9	6
31	C2	26	43	8	9
30	DE	34	20	11	5
36	North	44	32	11	6
25	Midlands	26	24	9	6
39	South	30	44	7	8
65	Married	65	63	9	7
20	Single	14	29	6	10
15	Widowed/Divorced	21	9	12	4
33	Child in h/h	16	36	4	7
16	Quality Reader	16	17	9	7
57	Popular Reader	50	51	8	6
29	None	37	38	12	9
29	Heavy TV	32	26	10	6
42	Medium TV	38	41	8	7
29	Light TV	30	33	9	8
38	Conservative	46	34	11	6
28	Labour	21	29	7	7
7	SLD	5	4	7	4
7	SDP	7	5	10	5
34	Thatcherists	30	37	8	7
54	Socialists	59	46	10	6

Source: MORI

On only two items of sexual behaviour, though, was there any significant difference between the sexes: 37% of women thought abortion was wrong compared to 33% of men. But women were more tolerant of homosexuality than men. Only 35% of them thought it morally wrong compared to 45% of men.

Policy makers might like to note one final result from our poll. There is a high degree of acceptance both of euthanasia and capital punishment. Only one in five people (22%) find either immoral: a grim finding indeed.

Strait-laced and Unlaced

Who, we wondered, are the puritans among us and who are the uninhibited free-thinkers?

We sought them out at both ends of the moral scale, finding our puritans among those who disapproved of practically everything on our list and our free-thinkers among those who found almost nothing on our list to be shocked at. On this basis, we found 131 puritans, making up nearly one in ten (9%) of the population and 99 free-thinkers, making up around one in fourteen people (7%).

Table 7–2 profiles these opposite types. But we were struck by how little was the difference in their make-up. Free-thinkers tend to be young, male, Southerners and they are twice as likely to be single as puritans. Puritans tend to be older, female and Northerners. But only one woman in ten is a puritan while one in twenty is a free-thinker. Between our Socialists and Thatcherists there was not a lot of difference in moral attitudes.

8

The British:
Drinking & Drugs

'THERE IS NOTHING WRONG WITH SOME DRUGS BUT SOME
THINGS THEY GET INTO, HEAVY DRUGS, IT JUST TAKES THEIR
MIND OFF OF IT. TRIPPING INTO ANOTHER WORLD, KNOW
WHAT I MEAN?'

We did not set out with the particular aim of focusing attention on
drugs or alcohol. We simply included each of them in a number of
our survey questions as possible causes of certain kinds of breakdown
and as sources of concern; and indeed as possible sources of pleasure
and enjoyment too.

But so worryingly high did they score on several counts that we
felt we had to give them a chapter of their own. Our respondents'
answers forced us to realize that in drugs and alcohol there lay
problems the depth and extent of which we had not anticipated.

Both forms of addiction were seen to have deeply harmful effects
on marriage. When we inquired what people thought were the 'main
factors' contributing to divorce, alcohol and drugs ranked very high.

From a list of fourteen possible contributory factors, alcohol was
rated the second most important cause of marriage breakdown and
drugs the third: 56% of our respondents thought alcohol a main
factor and 50% also thought the same of drugs. Only money problems ranked higher.

Drugs and alcohol were both rated significantly higher than what
might be thought more obvious problems within marriage, like sex,
children (both having them and being childless), working mothers
or in-laws.

When we turned to crime we found that drugs and alcohol again
rated as a 'main cause' and in even greater numbers than their

ranking among the factors in divorce. This time round, drugs were rated more important than alcohol. In a list of ten, only lack of discipline from parents was rated higher than alcohol and drugs as a main cause of crime.

The figures for the three most important causes were: lack of discipline from parents, 75%; drugs, 71%; alcohol, 62%.

People also rated drug and alcohol-related crimes among the most serious of all types of criminal behaviour. Only crimes of outright violence – sexual abuse of children, rape, terrorism, armed robbery and mugging – were rated higher. These scored between 96% and 81% when we asked which from a list people considered 'very serious crimes'. Next to those came driving when over the legal limit of alcohol at 78%; drug-taking followed at 58%. After these two came football hooliganism and burglary, which rounded off the list of crimes that more than half the population rated as very serious.

The other crimes on our list were strictly non-violent – evading taxes, for instance, and shop-lifting. It appears, therefore, that people associated alcohol and drugs with crimes of violence, the kinds of crime which they rate most seriously and of which they are most fearful.

8-1   Drinkers

British Public		Drinkers (50% = 100%)
%		
100	All	100%
48	Men	55
52	Women	45
37	15–34	38
29	35–54	31
33	55+	31
39	ABC1	48
31	C2	28
30	DE	24
36	North	34
25	Midlands	25
39	South	41
65	Married	64
20	Single	22
15	Widowed/Divorced	14
33	Child in h/h	30
16	Quality reader	20
57	Popular reader	58
29	None	25
29	Heavy TV	24
42	Medium TV	43
29	Light TV	33
38	Conservative	41
27	Labour	27
7	SLD	8
7	SDP	7
34	Thatcherists	38
54	Socialists	52

People, then, consider alcohol and drugs as serious factors in two of Britain's key social problems, crime and divorce. But that does not stop them cheerfully acknowledging their enjoyment of at least one of the two.

When we asked which of sixteen things – from eating fresh fruit to jogging – people had done in the previous two days we found that half, or 50%, had consumed an alcoholic drink.

That represented an increase of 4% on four years earlier when an identical question was asked and it revealed increased alcohol

consumption as almost the only consumer habit generally regarded as unhealthy which was on the rise.

We also asked which of a range of things people had done in the previous month and we found 46% had been to a pub and 12% to a wine bar, while 51% had had friends round to their own homes for a meal or a drink.

Drinking alcohol either alone or on social occasions in which it plays a central part can therefore be recognized as firmly built into the social habits of the British people.

Drug-taking, on the other hand, is not. Only a negligible 1% of our respondents said they had taken marijuana or any other drug in the previous two days, against the 50% who said they had taken an alcoholic drink.

That may, of course, be due to a reluctance to admit to an activity which is, after all, illegal. Even so we would not expect to get such a low response if drug-taking really were widespread.

That prompts a question. Are people more alarmed about drugs by reading alarmist stories about them than they need be, judging by the numbers who actually consume marijuana, cocaine or crack? When they blame drugs for crime and divorce, are people blaming a myth?

Alcohol consumption is certainly no myth. But its prevalence suggests another question. Why do people so freely consume what they hold responsible for some of society's most grievous problems? Do they believe they can handle it, even if others cannot?

These are unanswered puzzles. What is not in doubt, though, is the seriousness with which drugs and alcohol are seen as threatening dangers. Together they might even be held to contain the ingredients of a modern plague. If this sounds extravagant, it may seem less so if we compare the public perception of drugs with that of AIDS, which is often described as a genuine plague in the old-fashioned, even biblical, sense of that word. When we asked people to rate which of twenty-four issues concerned them most, drug abuse came fourth. AIDS came well below it, in eighth place.

9

Crime in Britain

'I DON'T AGREE WITH MUGGING. IF YOU ARE GOING TO COMMIT A CRIME, BORROW SOMEONE'S CAR, STEAL THEIR STEREO, BURGLE THEIR HOUSE. BUT DON'T DO NO ONE NO HARM. AS LONG AS YOU DON'T HURT PHYSICALLY, IT IS ALL RIGHT.'

Crime is the great fear that haunts the minds of the British people; above all, crime involving physical violence.

The fear spreads across sex, age and class barriers. Fear of violence is increasing at an extremely rapid rate, and it is most deeply felt by women.

We have already seen that crime was the issue which came top when we asked our respondents to rank a long list of worries according to the depth of their concern. That proved the importance of crime in general. But we wanted to know more. The law describes a huge catalogue of offences as criminal. Which did the largest number of people rate as genuinely serious and which were seen to be so by fewer people? And who or what did they hold responsible for the crisis of crime they perceived all around them?

There proved to be no doubt about which crimes were held to be serious by the most people. They were crimes of physical violence – especially sexual violence – and those where a threat of physical harm was at least implied.

We drew up a list of fifteen criminal offences, ranging from those which guaranteed the guilty very long jail sentences to others which would earn them only a minor fine, and we asked our respondents which, if any, they considered to be 'very serious crimes'.

There was virtual unanimity about which were the two most

I'm not mugging you sir – I just want to ask a few questions..

serious crimes of all. Sexual abuse of children was seen as very serious by 96% and rape by 95%. Those two crimes were regarded as so obviously serious that they formed a class of their own.

Terrorism, with a score of 87%, armed robbery (85%), mugging (81%) and driving over the legal limited of alcohol (78%) formed a second tier.

A third tier of three crimes completed the list of those rated as very serious by above half the people we questioned. They were drug-taking (58%), football hooliganism (52%) and burglary (51%).

Only one of these last crimes, football hooliganism, is by definition violent. But the other two carry with them at least a suggestion of physical harm, as drivers over the alcohol limit suggest death or injury to other drivers, passengers or passers-by. Drug-taking carries with it an image of addicts as desperate people who may be willing to rob at knifepoint to support their habit and are surely ready to destroy themselves in pursuit of it; while, though a burglar may only be after whatever valuables he can carry away with him, he may very well be willing to resort to violence if he is caught in the act.

There is a wide gap in public perception of their seriousness between those crimes that are clearly violent or associated with violence and those which are not. None of the remaining crimes on our list carried even a whiff of violence about them and none of them came near to being rated very serious by as many as half our respondents.

This was how non-violent crime was ranked: financial swindles in the City of London – 37%; discrimination on the grounds of race or sex – 31%; claiming State benefit to which you are not entitled – 31%; tax evasion – 24%; shop-lifting – 23%; avoiding fares on public transport – 9%.

The gap between violent and non-violent crime almost overwhelmed every other difference. But there were some intriguing smaller differences in attitudes.

Although child sex abuse and rape were universally detested, marginally more women, not surprisingly, rated both as very serious than did men (97% to 95% and 96% to 94%). Most other forms of violence more men rated very serious than women. Terrorism, for example, scored 89% with men to women's 85%. The exceptions were driving over the limit and drug-taking, both of which more women judged serious.

Fewer women than men rated non-violent crime as very serious. The exception was shop-lifting. One woman in four (26%) scored it as very serious compared with one man in five (20%). Can this be because shop-lifting is sometimes thought of as a 'woman's crime'?

Strangely, though, women were no more concerned about discrimination than men. Why should only 30% of women regard discrimination on grounds of race or sex as very serious compared to 32% of men when it is women who are much more likely to be victims of any discrimination there may be going?

Fewer young people take a serious view of money crimes than do their elders. Only 24% of 15 to 34-year-olds thought claiming State benefits you're not entitled to very serious against 40% of over 55s. Again, just one in twenty, or 5%, of the youngest age group believed avoiding fares on public transport to be very serious, against three times as many in the oldest age group, or 15%.

Young people are also the most likely to commit crimes, with 15 as the age with the highest criminal rate. Can it be that young people commit crimes for the simple reason that they do not believe there is anything wrong with many of the offences the rest of society regards as criminal?

Crimes of violence are not only the ones the British rate as most serious. It is also violent crime of which people are growing most rapidly afraid.

We wanted to know which crimes people feared most and what sort of day to day behaviour they might find frightening because of its potential danger to themselves. We chose our list so that it could be matched against an earlier survey and provide us with evidence of how the focus of fear might have been shifting.

Respondents were shown a list and asked which were fears 'you personally have'? This was how they answered.

9-1   Fears & Worries

Q   Which, if any, of these are fears which you personally have?

	1987 %	1989 %	Change ±%
Having my home burgled	60	58	−2
Having my home or other possessions vandalised	49	48	−1
Being mugged (ie attempted or actual theft of my possessions while still on my person)	38	48	+10
Being raped	26	41	+15
Being attacked in my own home	29	41	+12
Going out alone at night	37	36	−1
Using public transport at night	19	24	+5
Having one or more of my possessions stolen (not from my person)	24	21	−3

Source: MORI

The significance of these figures becomes clearer if we compare them with the figures of actual crime recorded by the police in England and Wales. In 1988 police recorded 3.7 million notifiable offences; 3.5 million, or 94%, were crimes against property and only 216,000, or 6%, were crimes of violence.

So it was realistic of people to put fear of having their homes burgled and their homes or other possessions vandalized at the top of the list, since these are the sort of crimes of which they were most likely to find themselves victim.

Fear of violence was, statistically speaking, less realistic, in the sense that there was much less likelihood of any individual being the victim of a violent attack.

But that only emphasizes the depth of the nation's dread of violence. For people to rank their fear of things which are so unlikely to happen to them as close as they do things they have a much greater chance of suffering demonstrates with vivid clarity how deep the fear of violence has bitten.

Another insight into this fear can be had by seeing how steeply it has been growing and in how short a time. The figures in our table show this very clearly. The first two crimes on the list showed little major change. Fear of burglary and vandalism stood at a similar level both times. But where violence was involved fear had leaped dramatically in only two years.

Fear of mugging jumped 10 points, from 38% to 48%; fear of attacks in the home was up 12 points, from 29% to 41%; fear of rape up 15 points, from 26% to 41%; fear of other forms of attack up 6 points, from 18% to 24%. Fear of going out at night alone stayed close to an already high 37%. But fear of using public transport at night had risen 5 points, from 19% to 24%.

The way fear has shifted reflects changes in the pattern of crime with uncanny closeness. Though movement in the figures on fear of crimes against property was slight between our two surveys, they showed that if anything fear had eased a little. In 1987, 60% said they were afraid of having their homes burgled, against 58% in 1989; while in 1987 49% said they were afraid of having their homes or other possessions vandalized, 48% did in 1989. Police figures coincide with that shift. They show that there was indeed a slight fall, of 5%, in recorded property crimes in the year between our two surveys.

Conversely, fear of violence has moved up in tune with an actual increase in violent crime. Offences of violence against the person rose by 12% between 1987 and 1989, very much the same shift as our surveys reveal had taken place in the levels of fear about violence over very much the same period.

Fear of violence is soaring above all among women. In every situation where violence threatens, it is the women of Britain who are becoming most afraid.

As we have seen, fewer women rate violent crimes like terrorism, armed robbery or mugging as seriously as men, except for the specifically sexual crimes of rape and child abuse. But when it comes to fearfulness about violent crime more women feel they have more to worry about than men. On no other question was the gap between men's attitudes and women's as wide as on this.

For obvious reasons, we would expect women to be very much more afraid of rape than men, as our survey showed they were by a factor of ten, 72% to 7%. But women's fears went much further than that. They felt they had more to fear than men from every kind of violent or potentially violent situation.

56% of women said they were afraid of being mugged, to 39% of men;
55% of women were afraid of being attacked in their own home, to 27% of men;
57% of women were afraid of going out at night alone, to 11% of men;
35% of women were afraid of using public transport at night, to 11% of men;
27% of women were afraid of some other form of attack, to 21% of men.

Nor, we must point out, were women being needlessly alarmist. Police figures show that sexual offences, most of them indecent assaults on women, rose 6% in 1988 while recorded rape rose by no less than 16%.

Women are thus left bearing a double burden. They are not only the frequent casualties of crimes against their own bodies, they are made to suffer a second time by virtue of the burden of fear they must bear as well.

So what has gone wrong? What do people really believe are the main causes of the crime wave they are concerned about so much and fear so deeply?

We asked our respondents which from a list they thought were the main causes of crime in Britain today. This was how they replied.

9-2   Crime in Britain Today

Q   Which of these factors, in your view, are the main causes of crime in Britain today?

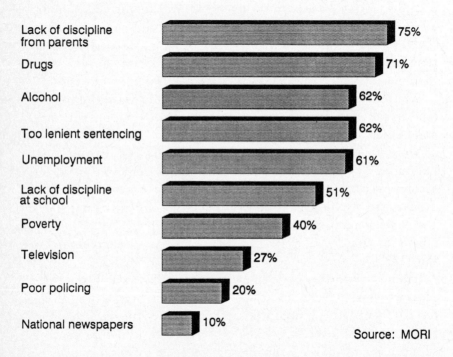

Lack of discipline from parents	75%
Drugs	71%
Alcohol	62%
Too lenient sentencing	62%
Unemployment	61%
Lack of discipline at school	51%
Poverty	40%
Television	27%
Poor policing	20%
National newspapers	10%

Source: MORI

There is a hierarchy of blame here but when we look at the figures more closely we find more than one pattern emerging.

There was, first, widespread agreement on the importance of alcohol and drugs as promoters of crime. As we have already shown, these habits are now seen as scourges so great as to amount to a virtual plague.

Discipline, or rather the lack of it, was seen to be making an important contribution to the crime problem. Older and middle-class people in particular tended to blame parents. The over-55s were most prone to lay the blame here, with eight in ten (84%) describing it as a main cause of crime, against two-thirds (64%) of the 15 to 34-year-olds.

Women and older people also stressed the importance of too lenient sentencing. On this issue the working classes agreed. More working-class respondents (C2s and DEs) rated it important (at 66% and 62%) than upper middle-class ABs, of whom 58% scored it important. The young were considerably less likely to agree.

The young also differed substantially from their elders on school discipline. Only 39% of the youngest age group gave lack of school discipline as a main cause of crime, against 62% of the over 55s. Women, in contrast with their sterner views on the two other questions of discipline, rated discipline at school less important at 49% than men at 53%.

We can contrast those who rate discipline highly with those who tend to put the blame on more general factors like unemployment and poverty.

More young people rated those two factors highly, as did more Labour supporters; 15 to 34-year-olds judged unemployment as the second most important factor of all in promoting crime, with only drugs narrowly ahead of it. Seventy per cent of this group rated drugs and 68% unemployment as key factors. The young also gave poverty a high rating: 47% said it was a main cause of crime compared to a third (33%) of the over 55s.

Labour supporters were likewise more inclined to blame unemployment and poverty for crime than were Tory. While seven in ten (70%) of Labour supporters rated unemployment an important factor, only just over half (53%) of Tories did. And 47% of Labour supporters cited poverty to only 35% of Tories. Tory supporters, on the other hand, put lack of discipline from parents 12 points ahead of Labour, lack of discipline at school 10 points and too lenient sentencing 8 points.

Perhaps, though, this division does no more than reflect the inability of anybody to come up with a persuasive explanation of the whole phenomenon of crime. Being unable to think of anything better, Tories fall back on their stock response, which is to place responsibility where they think it belongs – on the individual – while the Labour supporter, equally at a loss, falls back on his stock response, which is to blame society at large.

At least the Press can take some comfort from our findings, though not to the same extent television. It was part of Britain's mood in 1989 to blame both for falling moral standards, unacceptable sexual behaviour and excessive violence. Responding to this sense of unease the Government established a Broadcasting Standards Council to monitor the airwaves, and an inquiry into the conduct of the Press.

This looks suspiciously like the age-old habit of the powers-that-be to blame the messenger for the unpleasant messages he bears. But the British people are evidently not so inclined to blame the messenger. The national newspapers were rated at the bottom of our scale of criminal causes, with only one person in ten saying the Press was an important cause of crime, while one in four blamed television. For crime, at least, the Government must look elsewhere than the media for a scapegoat.

Crime stands as a paradox in our survey. It worries people deeply, and worry over criminal violence is soaring. Yet people have very mixed views on its causes and our findings produced no hint of a consensus. The people are as baffled as the experts.

We leave the subject with two paradoxes of our own.

How is it that a people which, as we have seen, rates having children outside marriage very low on its scale of things that are morally wrong, can at the same time be so ready to blame lack of discipline by parents for the crime wave it fears so much? For surely children raised in a stable marriage are more likely to be disciplined than those who are not.

Why do people rate lack of parental discipline higher as a cause of crime the older they get? After all, many of them must be the parents of today's criminals. Can it be that they have seen the error of their own ways only when it is too late to mend them?

British Marriage & Divorce

'YOU CAN GET MARRIED TO SOMEONE TODAY AND SHE COULD
BE LOVELY. BUT ALL OF A SUDDEN SOMETHING HAPPENS. AND
IT IS NOT ALWAYS THE WOMAN'S FAULT.'

Marriage and divorce, we have found, are very different: not the opposite sides of the same coin, but two different coins altogether.

Aspects of love like sex and friendship are thought by most people to be the key ingredients of a successful marriage. Material factors like money are held to be much less important. But when marriage turns sour and leads to divorce that judgement is turned upside down. Money problems now become far more important while sex slips well down the list of fatal distractions.

At the same time something else enters the picture, something which is not encountered at all in good marriages: The great modern plague we have several times identified, of alcohol and drugs.

Divorce doesn't just happen because the ingredients of successful marriage crumble and disintegrate. Marriage and divorce, our survey shows, are experiences made out of quite different ingredients.

We discovered this profound contrast when we asked our respondents first to say which items on a list were 'important in a successful marriage', then to tell us which from another list they thought were the 'main causes' of divorce.

How they answered is shown overleaf.

We now need to explore marriage and divorce separately and in some detail to get a better sense of the contrast between them. The ingredients of a happy marriage divide themselves neatly into a series of interlocking groups:

10-1   Success and Failure in Marriage

Q Now this is a list of things which some people think make for a successful marriage. Which of these, if any, do you think important in a successful marriage?

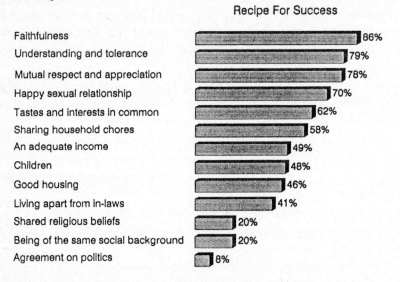

Recipe For Success

Faithfulness	86%
Understanding and tolerance	79%
Mutual respect and appreciation	78%
Happy sexual relationship	70%
Tastes and interests in common	62%
Sharing household chores	58%
An adequate income	49%
Children	48%
Good housing	46%
Living apart from in-laws	41%
Shared religious beliefs	20%
Being of the same social background	20%
Agreement on politics	8%

Q Here is a list of things which some people have said are the main contributing factors to divorce in Britain today. Which, if any, do you think are the main causes?

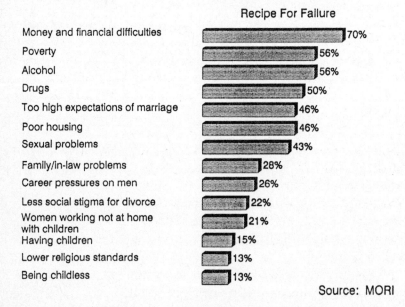

Recipe For Failure

Money and financial difficulties	70%
Poverty	56%
Alcohol	56%
Drugs	50%
Too high expectations of marriage	46%
Poor housing	46%
Sexual problems	43%
Family/in-law problems	28%
Career pressures on men	26%
Less social stigma for divorce	22%
Women working not at home with children	21%
Having children	15%
Lower religious standards	13%
Being childless	13%

Source: MORI

Sex, *represented in our list by faithfulness and a happy sexual relationship.* Faithfulness comes well ahead of sex itself. Men and women were at one on this, though men rated a happy sexual relationship marginally higher than women, by 4%. People evidently think that it matters less whether you find pleasure in your own bed than that you should not seek it in somebody else's. Looked at like this, faithfulness is not only a sexual issue. It also merges into our next group as a component of friendship.

Friendship, *represented by understanding and tolerance, mutual respect and appreciation, tastes and interests in common and sharing the household chores.* These are the common currency of ordinary friendship rather than blazing romance. They are the kind of thing that might bring people together without the cement of a sexual relationship to keep them close. People evidently believe that such companionship is just as important between husband and wife as it is between friends. Marriage means being friends with your partner as well as their lover.

(One cheering surprise here for women. Men actually rated sharing household chores a far higher priority than women did – at 66% to women's 51%. Does this reveal an untapped willingness among husbands to wash the dishes and put out the cat? Perhaps women should try asking more often. They might be gratified by the result; although men could always volunteer and spare women the embarrassment of making the first move.)

All the items in these first two groups were rated as important by more than 50% of our respondents. None of the remaining items struck as many as half our respondents as important to a successful marriage.

Material factors, *represented by an adequate income, good housing and living apart from your in-laws* (this last can be considered a material factor because it is related to the ability of couples to afford a place of their own). These three factors were rated important by from 41% to 49% of people, which put the highest-rated of them almost 10 points behind the lowest-rated item in the group we have labelled friendship.

It was noticeable that older people took more account of material questions than younger ones. Experience seems to have taught them how much an adequate income matters. Only 44% of the under 35s thought it was important, compared with 54% of 35 to 54-year-olds and 50% of the over 55s. People who were themselves married or living with a partner also knew how much money mattered: 51% of them rated an adequate income important to only 45% of singles.

Common attitudes, made up of shared religious beliefs, being of the same social background and agreement on politics. No more than one person in five rated any of these as important and fewer than one person in ten thought political agreement mattered. The exceptions were those who had been married but had become widowed, divorced or separated. They rated shared religious beliefs almost twice as important as single people, 29% to 16%. They also scored social background with approximately the same importance, at 28% to the young's 15%. Had experience taught them that religion still does count for something and that the pervasive and complex British feelings about class could still, even in the late 1980s, ruffle the calm marital scene behind the net-curtained windows?

(It may seem an intrusion to bring politics into marriage but it turns out that differing political views do go with different attitudes to marriage. Tory supporters rated most of the items on our list of ingredients in successful marriage more highly than Labour, the main exceptions being children and good housing which Labour supporters ranked higher than Tory. We couldn't help noticing, too, that SLD supporters laid particular stress on sharing household chores, putting it 6% higher than either of the major parties. SDP supporters, on the other hand, singled themselves out by laying more stress on agreement in politics than the supporters of any other party. More than twice as many of them thought this important than did their erstwhile colleagues of the SLD. We can't help wondering if this particular requirement makes it difficult for SDP supporters to find partners. If they confine their choice of spouse to fellow SDP supporters they will certainly be restricting their marriage chances.)

Children. They were rated important by almost half our sample (48%) but that ranked them well below sex and friendship, down among the factors in our relatively low-rated material group.

Does this mean the British don't like children, or only that they are ambiguous in their feelings about what children can do to marriage? Perhaps they fear that the patter of tiny feet can turn into a drumroll of disaster for marital bliss. It is at least suggestive that only 44% of women say they think children important in successful marriage. They may be particularly afraid that the appearance of babies in the bedroom will threaten their relations with their husbands. If so, they can be cheered by our finding that a majority of men (52%) say they think children important. It could be that the presence of children does more to make a success out of marriage than women dare to let themselves believe.

Divorce turns all this on its head. In successful marriages we found sex and friendship rated high while money matters rated relatively low. But when marriage turns into divorce it is the other way about. Now money matters most, and sex slides sharply down the scale of importance.

Financial difficulties and sheer poverty were seen to be the top two causes of divorce while poor housing – itself a consequence of financial problems – came only 10 points behind.

Sex problems, however, rated below even housing, coming seventh at 43% in our list of fourteen items. When marriage goes wrong, it is not in the bedroom that we should look for the causes.

Why is money thought to be so relatively unimportant in a successful marriage and so crucial when marriage breaks down and turns into divorce? One answer could be that people who are successful in their marriage are presumed to be sensible about living on whatever income they have. Good marriages take money in their stride and leave the partners free to concentrate on other matters, like friendship.

But it is tempting to see another and quite different pattern in our findings, a pattern focused around the crucial significance of alcohol and drugs. Neither alcohol nor drugs, of course, figured in our list of ingredients for success in marriage. It would have been pointless to include them since they are by definition problems, not bonuses, and we could have expected them to earn no more than a zero rating. But it was remarkable to find just how high they were ranked as ingredients in divorce.

Alcohol was seen as a main cause of divorce by 56% of people, exactly the same number as cited poverty, making alcohol second equal in significance among all causes; drugs came next to it at 50%.

Both alcohol and drugs were well ahead of sex and even further ahead of those other problems which it is so fashionable to talk

about these days, like working mothers who cannot be with their children because of their jobs or career pressures on men which prevent them performing properly as husbands.

Are, then, drugs and alcohol, and alcohol in particular, perceived to be the secret destroyers of marriage in our society? Are they in reality far more important than those other issues which people spend so much time fretting over, like bringing up children or not having any children to bring up? If so, we begin to find an unexpected pattern in our findings – alcohol and drugs helping to create destructive money problems on the one hand and destroying the expectations of marriage on the other.

It makes sense. Money difficulties are likely to arise where drink and drugs are already a problem. Addicts of both types need a lot of money to maintain their habits, and they are not likely to be the best of earners.

Addiction could also explain why too high expectations of marriage rated fifth as a cause of divorce at 46%, a place it earned especially from the judgements of no doubt rueful women, exactly half of whom rated it important, 8% more than men. Addiction to drink or drugs, then, forms the centrepiece of a pattern. On the one hand, it bolsters money problems, and on the other hand, disappointment, and perhaps contributes to sexual problems too.

Certainly this whole group of problems – money, alcohol, drugs, too high expectations, housing and sex – looms much larger than all the others. A clear 15 points separated our first seven factors from our second seven. Fashionable worries over children, for instance, came near the bottom of our list. Having children was seen to be scarcely more likely a cause of divorce than not having them (15% to 13%), and although working mothers who were not at home with their children were rated higher as a problem, still only around one in five people believed such lifestyles were an important factor in divorce. Career pressures on men were seen to be even more important, at 28%, and were seen to be so even by women, who put men's work problems three points above their own.

It also seems clear that people do not rate what we might call the disgrace factor very highly. They don't think that divorce has increased because less social stigma is attached to it in modern Britain or because religious standards are lower. People simply do not believe that divorce happens just because disgrace in the eyes of society or the church no longer automatically follows, thus making it harder to contemplate.

Good marriages, it appears, people believe to be made mostly out of love and friendship. But divorce is made out of something brutally different: above all, lack of money and addiction to alcohol and drugs. A successful marriage is like a story with a happy ending. Divorce is not the same story with a different ending – it is a different story altogether.

The British at Work

'I AM A DIRECTOR OF A COMPANY IN DARLINGTON.
FINANCIAL MANAGEMENT SERVICES. I CAN'T SHARE THE
DISILLUSIONMENT THAT OTHER PEOPLE DO. I HAVE FOUND
THAT I WORK SEVEN DAYS A WEEK AND GET NO TIME OFF. I
AM FLAT OUT.'

The British may like to grouse and grumble about the foreman or the chairman. But in spite of all the moaning, far more are satisfied with their jobs than otherwise.

What is more, through all the turmoils of the last decade their attitudes have scarcely changed. Never mind the industrial strife of the 'winter of discontent', the miners' strike and the Wapping confrontation. Forget the savage jump in unemployment to over three million in the mid-1980s and its slow decline since. Ignore the fierce contraction of Britain's manufacturing sector in the early years of the decade. Don't even give a thought to the yuppies and the new millionaires who have done so well out of those years either.

Britain's working population has doggedly sat through the whole experience – through the wildly different Prime Ministerships of James Callaghan and Margaret Thatcher – and emerged at the other end with their attitudes to work almost entirely unmoved and unchanged.

That high degree of satisfaction and its extraordinary stability emerged from one set of our survey findings which we were able to match against responses to an identical question in a 1976 survey.

In 1989, 82% of people in jobs were either very or fairly satisfied with what they did while only 10% were either fairly or very dissatisfied. In 1976 responses to the same question showed 83% on the side of overall satisfaction and 8% on the other side. This amounts to no significant change whatever over the intervening tumultuous years!

11-1 Satisfied with Our Work

Q Which of these statements comes nearest on the whole to what you think of your present (main) job?

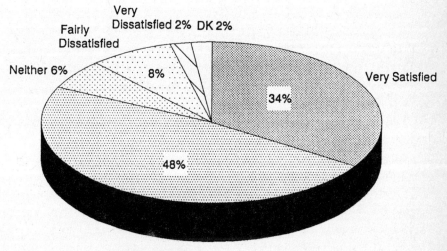

Very Dissatisfied 2% DK 2%

Fairly Dissatisfied

Neither 6%

8%

Very Satisfied

34%

48%

Fairly Satisfied

Base: All working (n = 798)   Source: MORI

From whichever angle we looked at the working population through the findings of our 1989 survey, the proportions of satisfied and dissatisfied remained much the same.

Those who scored themselves either very or fairly satisfied with their jobs rarely fell below 80% of their group and those who scored themselves fairly or very dissatisfied rarely rose more than a point or two above 10%.

More men were 'very satisfied' than women (36% to 32%), more over-55s than under-35s (41% to 32%) and more ABs than DEs (38% to 27%). But these differences tended to even out when we added in the 'fairly satisfieds' so that, for instance, the gap betwen ABs and DEs shrank from eleven points to only two.

The main differences can be seen best from our Net Satisfaction Index, the proportion in each group which said they were very or fairly satisfied, less the proportion which said the opposite. From the index we take only the most interesting results:

11-2 Job Satisfaction	(Net Satisfied)	%
	Men	74
	Women	71
By age	15–34	68
	35–54	77
	55 +	76
By union	Members	68
membership	Non-members	75
By party support	Conservative	77
	Labour	66

These are the kinds of difference we might expect to find. It makes sense to suppose that women, union members, Labour supporters and the young still get the rawer end of the jobs market and it would have been surprising to find them more satisfied with their jobs than their opposite numbers.

Much more surprising than that is the overall stability of attitudes. The Thatcher revolution has not made more British people satisfied with their work, as the Government might like to believe. But it hasn't made more of them dissatisfied either, as the Government's opponents might like to hope. In fact it hasn't made a jot of difference to people's attitudes one way or the other.

We also looked at work in another way, by asking to what extent people were interested and involved in the organizations which employed them and how much more involved they might like to become.

This showed that one in ten workers were not really interested in the company or organization they worked for, to whom 'it's just a job'. One in five, mostly women, liked to know what was going on but didn't really want to get involved. One in four liked to know what was going on and would like to become more involved. More than one in three liked to know what was going on and believed they were already involved.

Nearly one person in three, therefore, can be described as more or less indifferent to their employer's business except in so far as it affects them personally. They may want to know what goes on round their own workplace, but as for anything beyond that, like how the boss keeps the whole operation going, that's his business, not theirs.

At the extreme, a few (10%) turned up for the money only – 'it's just a job'. Twice as many (20%) were a bit more interested than that but not much. They were the ones who liked to know what was going on but didn't want to get too deeply involved. The rest, 70%, felt they did like to know what was going on in their business and, if they didn't feel they were involved already, wished they were.

We uncovered these attitudes by asking our respondents which of four statements came closest to describing their views about their current job. Here are the questions, along with the answers from the group of people within our survey who were in employment:

11-3   Involvement in the Job

Q   Please indicate which of these statements comes closest to describing your views towards your current job?

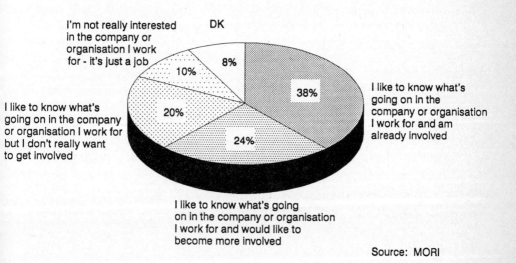

Source: MORI

Women were more lukewarm towards their employment than men. In spite of all the recent talk of women's advances in the world of work they were still more likely to regard their work as just a job and still much less likely to want to get more involved than they already were.

There may be a brighter side, though. It is possible that it is those women still stuck in second-class jobs who feel the lack of commitment, while those who have moved on and up the career ladder may feel as much commitment as men do. That could explain why almost as many women as men who did want to get involved in their work had succeeded in their aim.

11-4 Job Involvement (Gender)	Men %	Women %
1 ...it's just a job	9	12
2 ...I don't really want to get involved	17	25
3 ...I would like to become more involved	27	21
4 ...I am already involved	39	37

But it is the people with the best jobs – the ABs – who clearly are most into their work. More of them than any other group think they're already as involved in their organizations as they want to be. The DEs, the people on the bottom rungs of the employment ladder, are the least likely to be involved, and the least likely to want to be as well.

11-5 Job Involvement

(Class)	AB%	C2%	DE%
1 ...it's just a job	5	11	18
2 ...like to know what's going on but don't really want to get involved	13	24	29
3 ...like to know what's going on and would like to become more involved	21	27	27
4 ...like to know what's going on and am already involved	53	31	21

We can make an interesting link between people's levels of job satisfaction and their desire to get involved in their employer's business by looking at how groups of our respondents reacted to both sets of issues we have explored in this chapter.

When we do this we find that those who are most likely to be satisfied with their jobs are the ones most likely to be already involved with their organizations. Those who show the least satisfaction are also the ones most likely to regard their work as just a job.

People who regarded their work as just a job rated only 28% on our Net Satisfaction Index. Those who liked to know what was going on but did not want to get involved rated 71%. Those who would have liked to get more involved rated 72%. Those who were already involved rated 86%.

Obviously there are plenty of people around who can be described as reasonably satisfied with their jobs even though they have no wish to get more involved with their companies. They are happy enough to keep their organization's affairs at arm's length from their own.

But without question the most satisfied working people were the ones most involved in the organizations they worked for. There is a forceful message here for any employer who hankers after a more satisfied workforce.

Trade unions are not the issue they were ten or even five years ago. But if they still crop up anywhere it must obviously be in the world of work we are examining.

So how do trade unionists rate their jobs and their employers compared with those who are not trade union members? On our scale of Net Satisfaction, fewer trade unionists rated their job satisfaction highly than did those who were not union members: 68% of union members were satisfied against 75% of non-union members.

While fewer trade unionists claimed to think of their work as just a job (8% to 11%) more of them did not want to get more deeply involved in their organizations (24% to 19%).

However, 34% of trade unionists said they were anxious to get more involved against 20% of non-trade unionists. But then that could be because 41% of people who did not belong to unions said they were already as involved as they wanted to be, while only 32% of union members made the same claim.

These answers suggest a question. Is it because they are more likely than others to have low job satisfaction that people join trade unions in the first place? Or does joining a union make someone less satisfied with their job than they might otherwise have been?

This prompts another thought that may be worrying to trade unions. If people join unions in order to gain access to involvement – and therefore power in the organizations where they work – then clearly their membership hasn't paid off. Many more trade unionists are looking for involvement than non-trade unionists. And many more non-trade unionists believe they have as much involvement as they want already.

Do unions create problems for their members or solve them? Whichever answer is correct, trade union leaders need not despair. They are serving a cause which is by no means lost.

We asked people to respond to the statement 'Trade unions are essential to protect workers' interests.' More than half (58%) either agreed strongly or tended to agree. One in five (21%) were neutral. But only the same number (21%) disagreed strongly or tended to disagree. In spite of ten years which have seen unions hobbled by hostile legislation and their membership slide from 12 million to 9 million a powerful belief in their importance still lingers in the national consciousness.

We leave the subject of work on an uplifting note. Whatever else people may think about it we still believe we should do our bit. If the British ever admired shirkers, they surely do not do so today.

We asked people what they thought of the statement 'You should do as little work as you can get away with.' Only 6% agreed even mildly, 10% more were neutral, but 83% disagreed – 54% of them strongly. It is of interest that the 'shirkers' were only slightly more

	11-6	"You should do as little work as you can get away with"	
British Public			Agree (6% = 100%)
% 100	All		100%
48	Men		49
52	Women		51
37	15–34		43
29	35–54		27
33	55+		30
39	ABC1		24
31	C2		32
30	DE		44
36	North		42
25	Midlands		20
39	South		38
65	Married		63
20	Single		22
15	Widowed/Divorced		15
33	Child in h/h		39
16	Quality Reader		9
57	Popular Reader		67
29	None		27
29	Heavy TV		44
42	Medium TV		37
29	Light TV		19
38	Conservative		34
27	Labour		40
7	SLD		4
7	SDP		2
34	Thatcherists		40
54	Socialists		55

likely to be young, in the unskilled working class, in the north and Labour supporters. Of even greater interest is the fact that they are more likely than the average to be 'Thatcherists'.

Even if millions of people only go to work for the money and don't want to get involved in the affairs of the organization that pays them, most still believe they should do their bit in the factory or the office in return for the money they take home.

Anatomy of the Workforce

The workforce, as our survey revealed it, accounts for some 59% of the adult population. It is divided into full-time workers (i.e., those working 30 hours or more each week), who make up 42% of adults; part-timers (working between 8 and 29 hours), who make up 13%; and the unemployed (those wanting work but unable to find it), who make up 4%.

While adults as a whole split 48% to 52% between men and women, the adult workforce is not nearly so evenly divided between the sexes. Full-time workers are still men by a seven to three margin, while women still fill six out of seven part-time jobs.

Among adults who do not form part of the workforce are the retired (17%), non-employed housewives (14%) and full-time students (4%).

Nearly half (47%) of full-time workers are under 35 and one in nine (12%) are over 55. Six in ten men work full-time and only one in twenty-five part-time. But women workers are almost evenly divided between full-timers and part-timers. Just under a quarter (24%) work full-time and one in five (20%) work part-time. But this is not necessarily a matter of discrimination. Women who are mothers may prefer part-time jobs. That would explain why we found that over half of part-time workers have children in their household under 16 years of age.

Seven in ten of the unemployed are men and three in ten are women. Half of the unemployed are under 35 and two-thirds (65%) are unskilled. The proportion of unemployed is highest in the North.

Over half the unemployed (53%) are heavy television viewers. Over a quarter of them (27%) told us they would vote Tory if there was an election the next day, just over a third (37%) said they would vote Labour and three in ten said they didn't know or wouldn't bother.

11-7   The British Worker

British Public		Full–Time	Part–Time	Unemployed
%		(42% = 100%)	(13% = 100%)	(4% = 100%)
100	All			
48	Men	69	16	70
52	Women	31	84	30
37	15–34	47	41	50
29	35–54	41	41	33
33	55+	12	18	17
39	ABC1	43	40	21
31	C2	34	33	14
30	DE	23	27	65
36	North	34	39	44
25	Midlands	23	22	24
39	South	43	39	32
65	Married	69	75	40
20	Single	25	15	44
15	Widowed/Divorced	7	10	16
33	Child in h/h	37	52	32
16	Quality Reader	17	12	11
57	Popular Reader	58	53	69
29	None	27	36	28
29	Heavy TV	17	24	53
42	Medium TV	44	44	34
29	Light TV	39	32	14
38	Conservative	40	33	27
28	Labour	25	36	37
7	SLD	8	7	2
7	SDP	6	8	4
19	Trade Unionist	35	14	8
34	Socialists	39	30	31
54	Thatcherists	49	60	61

Source: MORI

12

Britain at Play

'WHEN YOU CATCH A FISH YOU GUT IT AND COOK IT, AND IT
IS FRESH, ISN'T IT? IT HASN'T BEEN FROZEN FOR SIX MONTHS.
IT IS JUST THE PLEASURE. YOU GET AWAY FROM THE NAGGING
WIFE AND AWAY FROM EVERYONE ELSE. YOU SIT THERE ALL
WRAPPED UP AND FREEZING. THERE IS NOTHING ELSE TO
BOTHER YOU BUT THE SEA.'

Our portrait of the British so far may have made them seem bowed down with grief and overwhelmed with worries; and so, up to a point, they are. Fears are real, worries do nag. But there is another side to this picture – a British face wearing a smile instead of a furrowed frown.

For the British enjoy themselves too. Whatever their problems may be, they manage to fit in a lot of pleasure around them. If the sky above is filled with clouds there are big, blue patches too. The sun peeps through the drizzle.

Britain's leisure is richly spent. People find time for a very wide range of alternatives to gloom. They are indulging every one of their tastes more and more, and the national reputation for philistinism – for preferring second-rate entertainments to the best – is totally misplaced.

More people go to art exhibitions than pop concerts and many more go to museums than football matches. We were not surprised to find, and nor will you be, that the most common form of spare-time activity is watching television. But what did you think would have come second? Going to the pub? Doing the garden? It was reading a book.

Forty years ago the poet T. S. Eliot defined the word 'culture' as including 'all the characteristic activities and interests of a people'. His own list read like this: 'Derby Day, Henley Regatta, Cowes, the twelfth of August, a cup final, the dog races, the pin table, the dart board, Wensleydale cheese, boiled cabbage cut into sections, beetroot in vinegar, nineteenth-century Gothic churches, and the music of Elgar.'

That list looks a little faded now. Perhaps Eliot would have included discos, wine bars and sports clubs if they had existed. Perhaps not. In any case he did not claim his list was exhaustive. He invited his readers to make their own. That is what we did. We drew up two lists, then invited our respondents to say which of the activities or items listed they had actually taken part in. From their answers, we believe, we have been able to draw an accurate picture of British culture, in Eliot's sense of 'all the characteristic activities and interests of a people', as it really is today.

We began by showing our first list to each of our respondents and asking them which of the things on it they had done in the previous month. Their answer, in order of popularity is shown overleaf.

Television is clearly the basic component of the national culture. When Eliot wrote, it was only available to a handful of well-off Londoners. Now satellite has made it accessible even to the remotest parts of Britain. As we have already seen, it is the most important source of information and opinion available to the nation. Now we can see that it is the most popular form of recreation too.

But it is by no means the universal monster it is sometimes said to be. People like their television. But it hasn't rendered them totally passive and helpless. They still find a great deal of time for other things – most notably, and perhaps most surprisingly, for books. Anybody who thought the electronic media would kill the printed variety was quite wrong. It just hasn't happened.

Reading a book came second in popularity to watching televison. More women read than men, the old more than the young and the middle class more than the working class. But the reading habit is widespread. In none of our categories had fewer than half of the people questioned, read a book in the previous month.

We can flesh out what we know about Britain's bookish habits from a special study made only a few weeks before our own. This showed, among other findings, that 73% of people had bought at

12-1   What We Do

Q   Which of these things have you done in the past month?

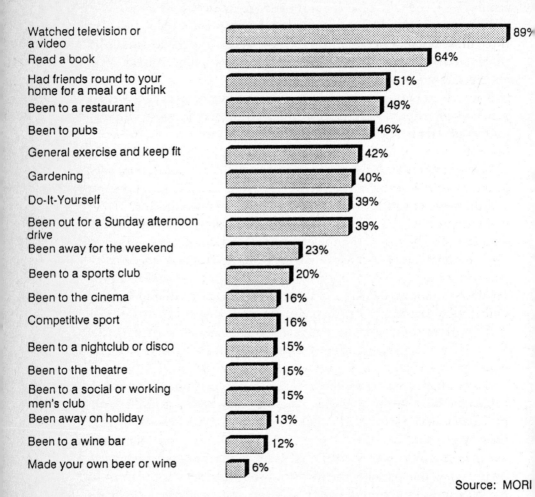

Watched television or a video	89%
Read a book	64%
Had friends round to your home for a meal or a drink	51%
Been to a restaurant	49%
Been to pubs	46%
General exercise and keep fit	42%
Gardening	40%
Do-It-Yourself	39%
Been out for a Sunday afternoon drive	39%
Been away for the weekend	23%
Been to a sports club	20%
Been to the cinema	16%
Competitive sport	16%
Been to a nightclub or disco	15%
Been to the theatre	15%
Been to a social or working men's club	15%
Been away on holiday	13%
Been to a wine bar	12%
Made your own beer or wine	6%

Source: MORI

least one book for themselves or somebody else in 1988. More than half the population had read ten books or more, and three in four had visited a bookshop (one in three more than ten times).

Book buying and book reading remain well-established cultural habits among the British. Television hasn't killed them off and it doesn't look likely to either.

Our survey should kill off another myth about television, which is that it has destroyed the nation's sociability. The story goes that the British are now so mesmerized by the box that they can hardly rouse themselves to switch it off for long enough to talk to their family, let alone take time to meet their friends.

This, too, is simply not true. After television and books, the next three most popular activities on our list were all sociable ones. The three were – having friends round to one's home, going to a restaurant, or going to a pub.

There were variations here too. Women were more likely than men to have friends round (55% to 46%), men were more likely to go to pubs than women (54% to 39%), and the young were more likely to go to pubs than the old (15–34-year-olds, 63%; over 55s, 25%); while middle-class people were more likely to be restaurant habitués than working-class (ABs, 63%: DEs, 32%).

Still, the habits of sociability, like the habit of reading, were strong in all our groups and showed no more sign of being destroyed by the demon-in-the-box than did the habit of reading.

Television and books are solitary pastimes. You don't need companions to enjoy them. Our second group of activities, which involved eating or drinking with other people, we called sociable. Our third group might be labelled self-help.

This group comprised general exercise and keep fit, gardening and Do-It-Yourself: activities which combine pleasure with improvement, whether of the body or the home. How much is done for pleasure and how much with gritted teeth we can only speculate. It is tempting to imagine that the 49% of men who said they had done DIY in the previous month (against 31% of women) were under pressure from their wives, or that the 58% of 15–34-year-olds who had taken exercise (against 26% of over 55s) were under pressure from their own vanity. But perhaps the pleasure was real, coming as much in the accomplishment – the flatter stomach, the sturdy new shelves – as in the activity itself. Whatever the motives, self-help activities are firmly established in British culture.

And they are moving rapidly up the scale. When we asked which of the activities listed people had done more frequently in the last twelve months than two or three years before, it was this self-help group which showed the most significant increase.

Everything on our list had gone up at least a little. Even wine- and beer-making had risen by a marginal 2%. Watching television and videos had gone up the most, by 21%. But general exercise and keep fit came next, alongside books, showing a 15% rise. Restaurant-going followed at 13%. Then came gardening and DIY at 11% and 10%, ahead of the other two sociable habits (having friends round and going to pubs) at 9% each. Taken separately, there is no great significance in the different rates at which these things have been moving up the popularity scale. Seen as groups, though, the self-help activities have been making markedly bigger strides than the sociable ones.

While we are on the subject of self-help, it is worth reminding ourselves briefly of people's changing attitudes towards food. If food seems out of place in a description of Britain's cultural life, we can only say that T. S. Eliot didn't think so and neither do we.

The point to be made here is the trend we have already noted towards healthier eating. We were able to compare a list of foods

which people said they had eaten in the previous two days with a comparable sample's response to an identical list four years earlier, in 1985. On almost every count we found they were consuming more of the healthier items, from fresh fruit to wholemeal cereals, and cutting down on unhealthy things like smoking. The main exception was taking alcoholic drinks, which had shown a small but marked rise of 4%.

Today's British culture contains a strong element of conscious self-improvement, including healthier food, to balance its heavy emphasis on more passive pleasures like watching television.

One other crime of which television is innocent is killing off other forms of live entertainment. Entertainments which require people to get out of the house to enjoy them are still very much alive and well:

16% of people had been to the cinema in the previous month. Most of them were young and middle-class: 31% of the 15 to 34-year-olds had been to the cinema but only 4% of the over 55s, and 23% of ABs had attended, as against only 8% of DEs. The cinema may have lost its attraction among those who formed its audience in the 30s, 40s and 50s, but it is carving out a significant new audience among the younger generation.

15% had been to a nightclub or disco. These, too, survive almost entirely on the custom of the young, almost one-third of whom (32%) said they had been to one or other in the previous month.

15% had been to the theatre: not, this time, a young people's preserve. Theatre-going was spread evenly through the age-groups, with 35 to 54-year-olds being marginally more likely to go than those older or younger. Perhaps surprisingly, it is not the preserve of the South either. To judge by the volume of publicity, everything theatrical seems to happen in London. But, if anything, Northerners at 16% can claim to be more regular ticket-buyers than Southerners at 14%.

If you ever wondered why there are so many traffic jams on your days off, you need wonder no more. Going for a drive on a Sunday is a very popular pastime, with 39% in our survey saying they had done it in the previous month, and most of that month was February. No wonder the jams are horrendous come July!

And as regards the timing of our survey, another of our findings looks all the more remarkable when we remember the dates we asked our questions.

It showed that 13% of people had been away on holiday in the previous month. We don't normally think of February as a holiday season but that is obviously changing. In terms of the population as a whole, our finding suggests that more than five million adults took themselves off somewhere away from home during the worst-weather month of the year. A lot of the young people who escaped (12% of the 15 to 34-year-olds) went skiing. But it was an even more popular holiday season with the over-55 generation, no less than 17% of whom got away, presumably taking advantage of off-season bargains to get as much winter sunshine as they could.

To complete our look at Britain's culture we wanted to discover how popular the more serious pastimes were, and also how popular were those entertainments which it is taken for granted actually are popular. Pop music, for instance, is by definition supposed to be just that – popular. But do more people take the trouble to go to concerts given by pop groups than to those given by orchestras? And what about football, supposedly the nation's number one spectator sport?

We probed this question by asking our respondents, 'Which, if any, of these have you been to in the past twelve months?'

From what we have already learned about reading habits, it was no surprise to find libraries at the top of this list. Nor, because of the enthusiasm of the young and even more the single, to find that cinemas came next.

What was much more unexpected was to see museums take third place. Perhaps they owed their position to dutiful parents towing their children round the dinosaurs on wet holiday afternoons? But that was not the case. Single people, it turned out, were more eager museum-goers than married or divorced. Middle-class people were more likely to go than working-class, but otherwise museums had a wide following.

The theatre followed close behind – the live action chasing the dead spectacle. Theatre owed its position to women and the middle class. It was not a favourite of the young. Middle-aged and older people liked theatre better. Older people were also slightly more enthusiastic than the young about art exhibitions, which came next, and middle-class people much more so than working-class (ABs 27%, DEs 8%).

It was only at this point in our league table that football matches

12-2 What We've Been To

Q Which, if any, of these have you been to in the past twelve months?

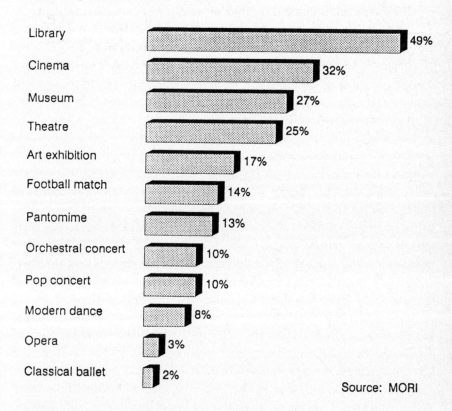

Library	49%
Cinema	32%
Museum	27%
Theatre	25%
Art exhibition	17%
Football match	14%
Pantomime	13%
Orchestral concert	10%
Pop concert	10%
Modern dance	8%
Opera	3%
Classical ballet	2%

Source: MORI

made their appearance. Who, thinking of Britain's reputation as a nation of football crazies, would have expected to see Britain's national game trailing behind art exhibitions in popularity and just ahead of pantomimes? We can put football's lack of appeal in an even more stark perspective by saying that as many men (25%) had taken part in a competitive sport themselves in the month before our survey as had been to a football match in the whole of the previous year.

Our survey was made before the Hillsborough disaster but the game's reputation for disorder and violence was already well established. If football can still claim to be the national game, it must be because television and the Press allow its fans to follow the game in safety and comfort.

Now we come to the question we posed above: which are more popular, orchestral or pop concerts? The answer is, neither. Both scored exactly the same, at 10%. Pop concerts were almost entirely the preserve of the young. Nearly one in four of the under 35s (23%) said they had been to one in the previous twelve months, while not a single person over 55 in our sample had been to a pop concert. Orchestral concerts were more favoured by the over 55s (13%) than the under 35s (7%) but that was not nearly so overwhelmingly dramatic a difference. Could it be that pop fans simply get tired of the decibels when they get older?

Modern dance, opera and classical ballet finished off our list. They are usually thought of as minority interests and that was how they rated in our survey. But that doesn't mean they are the interest of only a tiny handful. Though only from 8% to 2% of the population went to a performance of any of the three, that still reckons their live audiences in the millions and does not include the many who watched them on television.

By ranking these cultural activities in order of popularity, we may have given the impression that the nation is divided into exclusive groups of cinema-goers, football fans, opera buffs and so on. This would be quite wrong. Enjoyment of one thing by no means excludes enjoyment of another. People mix their pleasures freely and sometimes surprisingly.

Football fans, for instance, don't get all their thrills on the terraces. Half (50%) go to libraries and almost as many (47%) to the cinema. One in three (33%) go to museums and one in four to the theatre (23%) or pop concerts (21%).

Youngsters who go to pop concerts enjoy a similar spread of interests. Seven in ten (70%) go to the cinema, six in ten (59%) to libraries and more than a third to theatres (38%), art exhibitions and museums (both 35%), while almost as many (29%) go to football matches. Fifteen per cent even go to orchestral concerts.

Opera-goers, too, like a change. Almost as many of them (65%) as of pop fans go to the cinema. One in ten (12%) go to football matches and fractionally more (13%) are even prepared to cross the musical borderline and go to a pop concert.

Britain's culture is thriving, at any rate if you measure its health by the number of people who participate in a variety of the available public pastimes. However, we must qualify this breadth of participation in two ways.

First, just over one in ten of the population (12%) are particularly intensive cultural consumers. That was the proportion which attended at least seven out of the twelve activities we listed. These 'culturalists' were evenly split between the sexes, were younger than the average, were overwhelmingly middle-class (73%) and were less likely to live in the Midlands than the North or South.

At the other end of the spectrum was a much bigger and, we would say, sadder group, the 23% of the population, numbering almost 10 million people, who had been to none of the things on our list – not so much as a single visit to a library, a theatre, a pop concert or a football match. These unfortunates, the culturally deprived, tended to be slightly more female than male (25% to 21%), were twice as likely to be old as young (33% of the over 55s to 15% of the under-34s), three times as likely to be unskilled working-class as middle-class (36% DEs to 12% ABC1s), significantly more likely to be Midlanders (34%) than to live in the North (20%) or South (20%) and apt to be heavy television viewers (36%).

All the same, we can report that the nation is in no telly-induced trance. Its tastes mix watching and doing, 'high' and 'low' cultures, with a richness that contradicts the stereotypes of the British as divided between mindless lager louts and equally money-grubbing consumers. The mix we have found will not please everybody. Not enough football for some, not enough opera for others. But that is what we should expect in the culture of a whole nation. We doubt that, if T.S. Eliot were able to read our findings, he would be surprised – or disappointed.

13

Classy Britain

'I LOOK AT MYSELF AS LOWER THAN A LOT OF PEOPLE
BECAUSE I HAVEN'T GOT NOTHING. OK, I HAVE GOT
EVERYTHING THAT I NEED. I HAVE PUT IN A LOT OF HARD
WORK GETTING IT – NOT WORKING HARD, BUT A LOT OF
DUCKING AND DIVING. THERE ARE A LOT OF PEOPLE THAT
HAVEN'T GOT THAT. I THINK IT IS WRONG. PEOPLE WHO
HAVE GOT A LOT LOOK DOWN ON THEM. I THINK THEY ARE
YUPPIES AND SNOBS. I CAN'T GET ON WITH PEOPLE LIKE
THAT.'

Class is a fine old British obsession. Who am I? Where do I stand in life's great pecking order? Am I in the same class as the Joneses next door, or maybe a cut above them? Or – oh, horror! – are they perhaps a cut above me? If so what mysterious factors have conspired to bring me down? And what can I do about it? Take elocution lessons? Hang a pair of carriage lamps beside the front door? Hire a butler?

This is a caricature of the sort of questions that endlessly torment the British. But it is not a total distortion. The British do care about pedigree and manners, about going to the right school and speaking with the proper accent, about the clothes they wear and the street where they live. They still care about these things even after nine decades of the century of the common man and forty-five years in which Labour governments have claimed to iron out class differences once and for all from the Left and Tory governments to do the same thing from the Right.

Class, though, is not an exact science. There are no absolute and final answers to be had about life's pecking order. That, of course, is one of the fascinations of the class game. The rules are forever changing, the goal-posts are always on the move. Placings are highly subjective. If you believe you are working-class or middle-class, there are no definitive laws to say you're right or wrong. In class matters you are, in the end, what you think you are.

That, at any rate, is how we chose to approach the subject. We asked people to tell us which class they thought they belonged to and which class their parents had belonged to before them. Four things stood out from the answers. People are much more inclined to believe that they are middle-class themselves than that their own parents were. To call yourself working-class is no longer something to be avoided. On the contrary, at a time when by all objective standards more people than ever are entitled to call themselves middle-class, more people than before are perfectly content to call themselves working-class. Yuppies – people who are young and think of themselves as upwardly mobile – are not a media invention. They really do exist. But so do their opposites, the infinitely less glamorous downwardly mobiles. There are not so many of them but we still found plenty of people willing to admit that they were on the slide down the class ladder.

It is extraordinary how tenacious ideas about class are and how long the same kinds of argument have been going on. Notions common in the eighteenth century are still very much alive and well today.

Dr Johnson described one version of class differences like this: 'We are, by our occupations, education, and habits of life, divided almost into different species, which regard one another, for the most part, with scorn and malignity.'

You can hear that very same scorn and malignity in the voice of one of the people we talked to: 'The middle-class people are those I would say who are just about living on an inherited income. And the upper-class people are the multimillionaire people who have homes all over the world and yachts and that kind of thing, who are such a strata above what I have experienced in life as to be on a different planet. And there are a lot more of them than you realize.'

'Different species', said Dr Johnson. 'Different planets', said our interviewee. Different words, but the drift in both cases is the same. You are what circumstances have made you and the gap between you and somebody whom circumstance has assigned to another class is all but unbridgeable.

There is another way of looking at class differences and that is by birth. We are who our relations make us.

Oliver Goldsmith, a contemporary of Dr Johnson's, put it with classic simplicity: 'One man is born with a silver spoon in his mouth, and another with a wooden handle.'

We can catch echoes of that same distinction from another of the people we talked to: 'My wife's parents – I can't get on with them. They have a nice place with plenty of money. They aren't even allowed in my house. My mother-in-law comes and I won't let her in my house. I think she is looking down at me all the time. I can't stand that. They invite me to Sunday dinner. I can't go. I feel out of place.'

Wooden handle, you might say, meets silver spoon.

Lifestyle and relationships were the contrasting ingredients in those two different varieties of class definition. But both had one ingredient in common: money. Money put middle- and upper-class people on different planets, according to one of our interviewees, and money made the other feel out of place with his mother-in-law.

Money plays a constant but shifting part in Britain's class system.

In some people's eyes you can count yourself of very superior class if you happen to be the offspring of a duke, even though you are flat broke, while the same people might call a billionaire common if he spoke with the wrong accent. Money matters, but it is not the whole story.

From this taste of the complexity of class it must be obvious that if you want to discuss the subject with any coherence at all you must adopt some standards and definitions, otherwise you will get utterly lost. That is what the research industry has done. In its system money plays no direct part. Though it is obviously one determinant of status, what you do to earn it is more important than how much you earn. A vicar on £5,000 a year and a QC on £500,000 both rate as Grade A, because they are both qualified practitioners of a recognized profession.

The system divides the nation into six such grades: A, B, C1, C2, D and E. The Es are the easiest to define. They are people – like single parents, the unemployed and pensioners – who live entirely off State benefits. If the same people were to have any other source of income, such as a company pension, they would cease to be Es.

The other grades are perhaps easiest to understand when they are applied to an occupation that grades itself, like the military. Lieutenant-Colonel to Field Marshal makes you an A; Captain to Major, B; Sergeant to Lieutenant, C1; Lance-Corporal to Corporal, C2; Private, D; Retired Private on State benefits, E.

That is straightforward enough. If you work in the transport industry, though, your grading may seem a shade more arcane. A senior airline pilot and the captain of a merchant ship of more than 5,000 tons is an A. The captain of a smaller ship is a B. A driving instructor is C1. The driver with an HGV licence is C2. But someone who drives a local delivery van rates only a humble D.

Like any other class system, this one contains much potential for dispute, if not dismay. Why should a driving instructor rank in the same grade as a sister in a small teaching hospital? Or why should a student teacher be graded C1, while another student living at home with his father, who just happens to be a bishop, is an A?

The answer is that we live in a complex world. Any attempt at universal classification must cram everyone in somewhere and the result will look odd or arbitrary to someone. The research industry's system tries to impose a form of order that combines qualifications with position and earnings and assigns people who have none of these, like full-time housewives and other non-working family members, to the same status as the head of their household.

The system's particular usefulness at this point in our survey was to provide a standard against which to check people's opinions of themselves. When they say they are middle-class or working-class we can measure their subjective judgement against what they have also revealed to us about themselves in terms of their qualifications, jobs and so on. It is that information which enables us to plot their place precisely in the research industry's system of class gradings.

One other point to bear in mind. In conventional class terms, the research industry's system recognizes only the middle and working classes. C1s to As (sergeant to Field Marshal) are middle-class; C2s and Ds (private to corporal) are working-class, and so are State-supported Es.

The curious might like to know why the system does not recognize an upper class. This is for the very simple reason that such a class, however defined, would be too small to make a significant impact on statistical inquiries covering the whole nation. Even the holder of the most ancient and exalted dukedom in the United Kingdom of Great Britain and Northern Ireland must therefore accept middle-class status within the system.

We began our investigation by asking people to declare their own class affiliation, though we framed our question with the tact that seemed necessary for such a delicate inquiry: 'Most people say they belong either to the middle class or the working class. If you had to make a choice would you call yourself middle-class or working-class?' The answers were: 30% middle-class, 67% working-class, 3% don't know.

There were no differences between the way men and women rated their class standing. But young people were more ready to call themselves middle-class than their elders.

13-1 Self	15–34 years	35–54	55 +
	%	%	%
Middle-class	33	31	26
Working-class	63	65	72

People were also more willing to call themselves middle-class than they were to assign their parents to the same class.

We asked: 'Which social class would you say your parents belonged to when you started at primary school?' – 21% said their parents were middle-class, as against the 30% who said they were middle-class themselves; 75% said their parents were working-class, against the 67% who said they were working-class themselves.

13-2   How We See Ourselves and How Others See Us

Q   Most people say they belong to either the middle class or to the working class. If you had to make a choice would you call yourself middle class or working class?

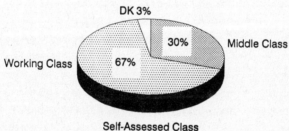

Self-Assessed Class

Q   What is the occupation of the head of household? Position/rank/grade? What type of industry/type of firm? What are the head of households' qualifications/degree/apprenticeships? How many staff is the head of household responsible for?

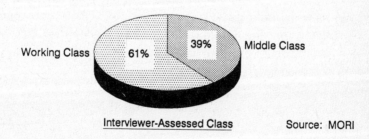

Interviewer-Assessed Class   Source: MORI

Again, the young were more likely to think of their parents as middle-class than their elders were.

13-3 Parents	15–34 years %	35–54 %	55+ %
Middle-class	26	15	21
Working-class	71	82	74

These findings confirm the accepted view that the old-fashioned working class, in cloth cap or headscarf, is on the way out and is rapidly being replaced by a new breed of well-dressed, home-owning, car-driving, holiday-taking middle-class folk. The greater willingness of younger people to call themselves and their parents middle-class supports the sense of a general drift through the generations towards acceptance of middle-class status.

But there is something pulling in the opposite direction as well. The middle class is growing, both objectively in terms of changing occupations and subjectively in the perceptions of younger people. But paradoxically the inclination for people generally to describe themselves as middle-class has not grown. Indeed, the exact opposite is the case.

As we have seen, 30% of the people we surveyed were willing to describe themselves as middle-class and 67% as working-class. But measured against the research industry's system of class identification, a lot of people assigned themselves to the wrong class.

By the industry's criteria, our sample broke down like this: roughly four in ten (39%) of all the people we interviewed were ABC1s, or middle-class. And six in ten (61%) were C2s and DEs, or working-class. So eight per cent fewer people called themselves middle-class than actually were, whilst six per cent more people called themselves working-class than actually were.

The mismatch can be put another way. Sixteen per cent of working-class people called themselves middle-class. But only just over half of middle-class people called themselves by their right class title. Just 51% of ABC1s said they were middle-class, while 46% assigned themselves to the working class.

Now of course we would expect quite a number of people to get their own status wrong. The research industry's system of classification is not widely known and it was not explained in detail to the people who answered our questionnaire. A student teacher could hardly be expected to know that he ranked in a different class from the student son of a bishop. Our respondents were only asked to place themselves in the class system, not tell us where they belonged in the research industry's hierarchy of class.

But it is at least intriguing that, at a time when it is a cliché to say the middle class is expanding and the working class disappearing, so many should prefer to assign themselves to the lower grade than the higher. It becomes all the more intriguing when we make comparisons with the past.

Class is one of the few things on which we actually can make direct comparisons with opinion research dating back several decades. Gallup, the grandfather of all polling firms – more than fifty years old against MORI's stripling twenty – was asking people what class they belonged to as far back as the 1940s.

Their approach then was slightly different from ours now. In 1949 they put their question like this: 'If you had to say what social class you belonged to, which would it be?' Gallup classified responses into a wider choice of replies than is done today. This was the answer it got:

13-4 Self-Assessed Social Class (1949)

Class	%	
Upper	1	
Upper middle	7	
Middle	29	All = 53%
Lower middle	16	
Working	43	
Don't know	4	

Different questions will, of course, produce different answers. But what we find fascinating is that forty years ago far more people assigned themselves to the middle class and far fewer to the working class than do today. And that was long before the explosion of white-collar jobs, home-owning, car-driving, share ownership and all the other indicators that are taken to show Britain is becoming more and more a middle-class society. Forty years ago only 43% of people called themselves working-class and 53% middle-class, against today's 67% and 30% respectively.

We can only speculate as to why fewer people should want to call themselves middle-class nowadays when many more of them, by any objective standards, actually are middle-class. The form of the Gallup poll forty years ago is itself interesting. Note that while it makes one undifferentiated mass out of the working class it offers four alternatives above – lower middle, middle, upper middle, upper. It is almost as if the question was designed to throw respondents a lifeline to help them climb out of the pit of working-class identity. Perhaps in those days the term working-class was not just a descriptive phrase but, to some people at least, a term of abuse, almost an insult.

A clue as to how differently people look at these things now was given by one of the group we talked to in Yorkshire. We were discussing class when he burst out with this: 'People like to put a label on things and say we are middle-class or upper-class and God knows what. At the end of the day you go out and work, so you are working-class.'

That may be the simplest and the best explanation of why 67% of people today rate themselves working-class against only 43% in Gallup's survey forty years earlier. If you work you must be working-class. And calling yourself that is no longer something to be coy about. It is a badge of honour, not of shame.

Whatever significance people may attach to being working-class or middle-class, there is no doubt a lot of them believe they are on the move in one direction or another through the class system.

Almost one person in every three (29%) described themselves as mobile: 22% said they were upwardly mobile and 7% downwardly mobile. It was the young who were most likely to think they were on the way up: 30% of 15 to 34-year-olds called themselves upwardly mobile against 25% of 35–54s and only 10% of the over 55s.

Here, of course, is where we look for the fabled yuppies. One of our London group thought he could spot a yuppie a mile off: 'The way they dress, the way they speak. They've always got their car phone or their portable phone with them.'

But that is the cartoon version of only one tiny part of the population that believes it is on the up escalator of class. They are the power-dressed, power-lunched high earners from the wheeling and dealing financial trades.

Upward mobility goes far wider than that. We cannot give you a neat caricature of the whole group. But we can tell you what its main characteristics are. As well as being young, an upwardly mobile person is more likely to be single than married or divorced (32% single, against 21% married and 15% widowed, divorced or separated) and slightly more likely to be a man than a woman (24% men, 20% women).

He is just as likely to read a popular as a quality newspaper (23% pop, 24% quality) and he does not watch a lot of television (30% are light viewers and only 15% are heavy). When it comes to politics Labour is his least favourite party. The upwardly mobiles make up 26% of Conservative support but only 18% of Labour's, which they also rate lower than either of the centre parties.

One other characteristic of the upwardly mobiles deserves a mention. People who believe they are rising up the class ladder also tend to believe their parents were upwardly mobile too: 46% of those who described themselves as upwardly mobile middle-class described their parents in the same terms and so did 44% of those who called themselves upwardly mobile working-class. Perhaps the claim to upward mobility is an inherited characteristic.

If it is, then perhaps downward mobility is too. More people who called themselves downwardly mobile middle-class put their parents in the same category than in any other class bracket. So did those who called themselves downwardly mobile working-class.

Besides this, the downwardly mobiles do not seem to have any very strong characteristics. In every category, from their political views to their newspaper reading, they huddle around the 7% mark, which is their share in the whole adult population.

Some people have always been tumbling down the class ladder while others have been clambering up it. It did not surprise us to have confirmation of that, though we were surprised that so many people were willing to admit they were on the way down.

Would people have been so frank forty years ago if Gallup had asked them? It could be that the very willingness of people today to say they are going down in the world is, like their readiness to call themselves working-class, a sign of a general easing of class barriers and class distinctions.

14

Britain & the World

'THE FRENCH SLAG OFF THE BRITISH AND THE BRITISH SLAG OFF THE FRENCH. WITH THE TUNNEL, MORE AND MORE PEOPLE WILL GO THERE. THEN PEOPLE WILL GET EVEN MORE ANTI-FRENCH.'

The British are beginning to perceive the world beyond their own shores in a new light. Quietly and without much public drama a deep re-evaluation of the nation's place in the world has been taking place, as those who remember Britain's high days of Empire and the Second World War grow old and die.

International issues, as we have already seen, are not of great concern to most British people. When we inquired about what things did concern them, defence, foreign affairs and relationships with America came at the very bottom of the pile. The Common Market came only a few notches higher. Even nuclear weapons ranked well below pensions and social security.

But if questions like these are not at the front of the national mind that does not mean people have no opinions at all or are incapable of changing their views about the world as the world around them changes. It is clear, for instance, that there is wide acceptance of Britain's diminished status as a world power. When we asked people to respond to the blunt statement, 'Britain has lost its role in the world', exactly half (50%) either agreed strongly or tended to agree, while only 27% disagreed.

So how do people see Britain's place today, now that they know their country no longer plays a dominant world role?

A few years ago the answer would have been broadly this. America and the Commonwealth – the countries of the old Empire – were most important to Britain. Europe was far less important, and the Soviet Union was the superpower which posed the greatest threat to peace. Now some of these attitudes have shifted and others have reversed.

We asked which between Europe, the Commonwealth and America was 'the most important to Britain' and we were able to compare the response with attitudes to the same question expressed on three other occasions over the previous twenty years.

The result reveals a sea change in thinking. Europe has more than doubled in importance to the British in two short decades while the importance of the Commonwealth and America have both shrunk sharply.

14-1   Most Important To Britain

Q Which of these - Europe, The Commonwealth, or America - is the most important to Britain?

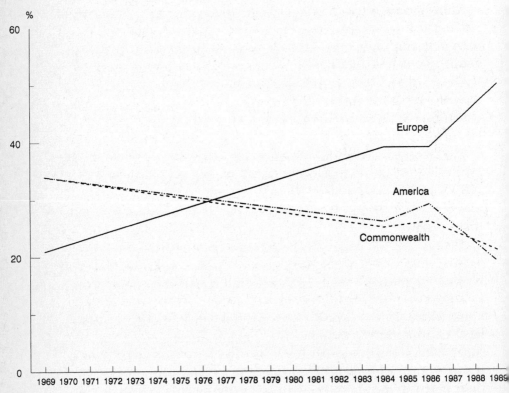

Source: MORI

146

The shift has come about in two phases. Europe first jumped in importance during the 1970s, when Britain's wrangle over membership of the Common Market was finally settled after a lengthy argument and a clinching referendum. Then it jumped a second time even more abruptly in the late 1980s as people became aware that 1992 had been fixed as the date for full integration between the markets of the twelve member countries.

The British, though, have not yet been won over heart and soul to the Common Market. When we asked whether people thought the Common Market was a 'good thing' for Britain, fewer than half (44%) agreed and only 11% agreed strongly. British indifference was underlined soon after our poll by the elections to the European Parliament, when Britain's turnout was the lowest in Europe. All the same, half-hearted though they may be, people have come to terms with Europe's importance and learned to score it higher and score America and the Commonwealth correspondingly lower.

More recently, another change in perceptions has been taking place. The British have become less worried about the Soviet Union's warmongering intentions and more so about America's, and this before the remarkable changes in Eastern Europe at the end of 1989.

Over a short three years, opinion about which superpower represents the biggest threat to world peace has been moving rapidly. America now looms as a larger threat than it used to and Russia as less of one.

This emerged from the response to a question which was first asked in 1986 and which we repeated in our survey. It was this: 'Which of the superpowers, if either, contributes the biggest threat to world peace in your view, the USA (the Americans) or the USSR (the Russians)?'

As table 14.2 on page 148 shows confidence in Russia has clearly grown while confidence in America has fallen, as has willingness to blame both powers equally. Russia is still regarded by more people as a greater threat than America but the gap has narrowed to the point where, if it was only men's opinions that counted, it would have disappeared completely. Men in our survey rated both the superpowers on a par with each other (America 29%, Russia 30%). It was women who swung the balance in favour of America. Nearly three in ten women (38%) saw Russia as the greater threat and only one in four (23%) America.

14-2   Threat to Peace - 1

Q   Which of the superpowers, if either, contributes the biggest threat to world
peace in your view, the USA (the Americans) or the USSR (the Russians)?

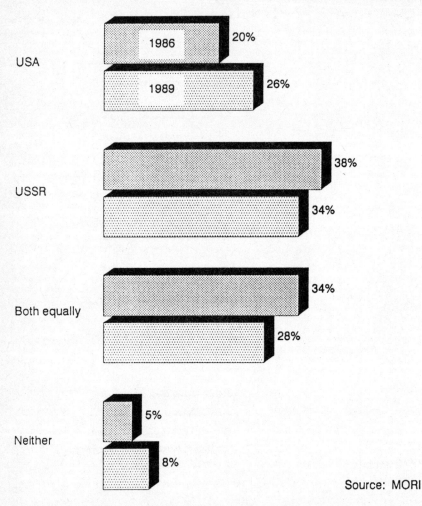

USA
1986   20%
1989   26%

USSR
38%
34%

Both equally
34%
28%

Neither
5%
8%

Source: MORI

Scepticism about America was stronger among middle-class people
than working-class. Readers of quality newspapers actually perceived
America as a greater threat than Russia. So did trade unionists and
supporters of the Labour Party. The figures are opposite.

Why the change? Why do the British seem to trust the American
nation less than they used to? Is it the Reagan factor? Certainly, the
slide in Britain's confidence coincides with the Reagan years and the

14-3 Threat to Peace - 2

Q Which of the superpowers, if either, contributes the biggest threat to world
peace in your view, the USA (the Americans) or the USSR (the Russians)?

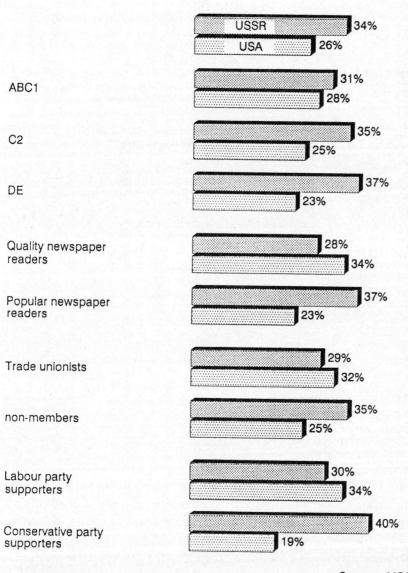

	USSR 34%
	USA 26%
ABC1	31%
	28%
C2	35%
	25%
DE	37%
	23%
Quality newspaper readers	28%
	34%
Popular newspaper readers	37%
	23%
Trade unionists	29%
	32%
non-members	35%
	25%
Labour party supporters	30%
	34%
Conservative party supporters	40%
	19%

Source: MORI

close relationship between the former President and Mrs Thatcher has done nothing to stop it. Or is it the Gorbachev factor, that new openness in politics combined with a readiness to talk arms control which has so successfully wooed opinion in other parts of Europe, especially West Germany? Or is there something else entirely going on?

It certainly isn't that the British have any less liking for the American people or for America as a place to visit. Both scored higher marks in our survey than they had done a few years earlier. But America as a place to settle in or learn from, or as a role model for the British themselves – these notions have plunged in people's estimation.

We uncovered these shifts in attitude by asking people to tell us whether they agreed with a series of statements that moved from the human and personal to the social and general.

The first statement was: 'I like Americans as people'. Seven out of ten (69%) agreed with that and liking for Americans was pretty constant and widespread throughout our groups. One variation is worth noting, though. Slightly more men said they liked Americans than women (71% to 67%). Otherwise there were no statistically significant differences by age, class, region, or even politics. Labour and Tory supporters were just as likely as each other to like Americans.

The next statement was: 'I would like to go on holiday to America'. Among people generally this was almost as popular an idea as liking Americans as people. Again, almost seven people in ten agreed (66%). Again, men were slightly more enthusiastic than women, 69% of them agreeing that they would like to holiday in America against 63% of women, and again, there was no other difference by age, class, region or politics.

There were some wider variations between other groups, though. Many more young people than old agreed (among the over 55s, in fact, slightly more people would prefer not to go on holiday to America at all – 48% to 50%) and significantly more middle-class people than working-class would like to travel there. However, more trade union members than non-members (71% to 66%) were attracted to the idea of crossing the Atlantic for a holiday.

These two statements both attracted majority support and support for both had gone up since the last time they had been put to the test of a survey. In 1986, 66% had said that they liked Americans as people compared with 69% in 1989, and 64% had thought they would like to go on holiday to America compared with 66% the second time round.

But our three other statements all failed to win agreement from a majority and, even more significantly, support for each of them had dropped sharply over three years.

Here are the statements and the level of support they attracted:

14-4   Attitudes to America - 1

Q Here are some things that have been said about America and the Americans. On balance, do you agree or disagree with each one?

I think we can learn a great deal in this country from America

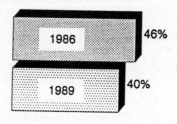

I would like to live in America if I could not live in Britain

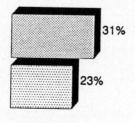

We would be better off if we were more like the Americans in many respects

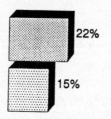

Source: MORI

151

We can see even more clearly the gap between attitudes towards America on the personal and on the social levels if we look at the 'net agreement' each of our statements produced in the 1989 survey, that is, the percentage of those who agreed with the statements less the percentage of those who did not.

The contrast between the extent to which the British like Americans and their country and the extent to which they admire America as a nation is striking. More than half agreed with the first sort of proposition; a good many more than half disagreed with the second.

14-5 Attitudes to America - 2

Q Here are some things that have been said about America and Americans. On balance, do you agree or disagree with each one?

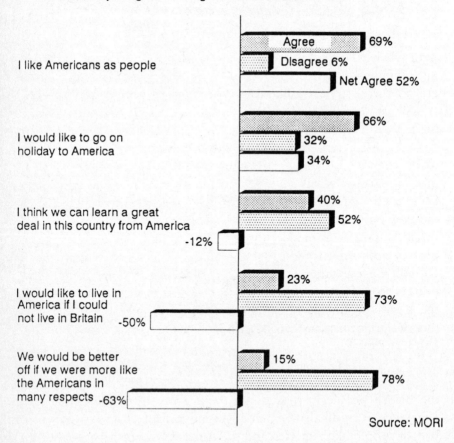

Source: MORI

In tandem with this reduced respect has come a more guarded judgement of America as a superpower. Fears that it could pose a greater threat to peace than Russia are considerably on the increase.

We are not seeing in all this a set of knee-jerk reactions. People do not either like or loathe everything American. Worries about America as a threat to world peace do not lead people automatically to downgrade Americans and their nation. Our respondents were discriminating. It was notable, for instance, that while more men consistently rated American people and their country higher than did women, more men than women also rated America as a greater threat to peace. Similarly, trade unionists and Labour party supporters both saw America as a greater threat to peace than Russia without having other anti-American attitudes. Fewer Labour supporters than Tory, for example, disagreed with the proposition that the British would be better off if they were more like Americans (net disagreement was −65% among Tories, against −56% among Labour).

It may be that the Gorbachev factor is working its magic among the British people in persuading them away from their American allegiance. It could also be that a Reagan–Bush factor is at work too. British people like America and the Americans, but perhaps they do

14-6   Profile of the "Anti-Americans"

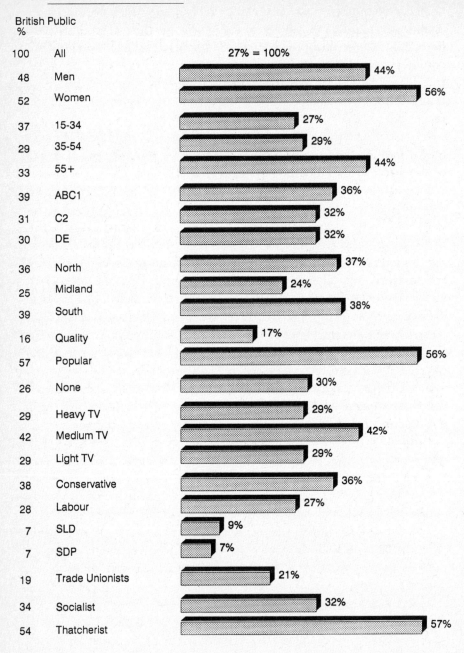

British Public %		27% = 100%
100	All	
48	Men	44%
52	Women	56%
37	15-34	27%
29	35-54	29%
33	55+	44%
39	ABC1	36%
31	C2	32%
30	DE	32%
36	North	37%
25	Midland	24%
39	South	38%
16	Quality	17%
57	Popular	56%
26	None	30%
29	Heavy TV	29%
42	Medium TV	42%
29	Light TV	29%
38	Conservative	36%
28	Labour	27%
7	SLD	9%
7	SDP	7%
19	Trade Unionists	21%
34	Socialist	32%
54	Thatcherist	57%

Source: MORI

not like much that has been happening to that nation in recent years.

There is another possibility, of course. Falling British respect for America as a model or a place to live – as some kind of ideal society, or one at least to admire – may be the result of increased British confidence in their own society. Perhaps the British no longer feel they should emulate America because they believe they are now doing things much better their own way than they managed in the recent past.

It was an American statesman, Dean Acheson, who said of Britain that it had lost an Empire but not yet found a role. On the evidence of our survey that bald statement needs qualifying.

Britain has indeed lost an Empire and the British are content to recognize that fact. They no longer believe that the remaining ties with those now independent nations which were once coloured pink on every British schoolchild's map are very important to them. They like America and the Americans but they are not overwhelmed by the combination. The people and their country, yes; but the society and its policies, far less so. At the same time suspicion of Russia is decreasing. People still regard it as a greater threat to peace than America, but less strongly than they used to. They are fast recognizing that Europe's importance to Britain now far exceeds the importance of old ties with either America or the Commonwealth.

The British accept that they have lost an Empire across the oceans. But they are now slowly settling into a new role in the world, as a nation committed to the Europe that lies across the Channel.

15

British Possessions

'IF YOU ARE GOING TO SLAVE YOUR GUTS OUT ALL WEEK,
YOU DESERVE TO BE ABLE TO DO A HOBBY OR GO OUT TO
HAVE A DRINK WITH YOUR MATES, RIGHT? IF YOU ARE GOING
TO GO AND WORK ALL THAT WEEK AND YOU STILL CAN'T
AFFORD TO DO THAT, YOU ARE NO BETTER OFF. YOU CAN'T
DO IT.'

What people choose to spend their money on may seem a poor guide to their attitudes and beliefs. Are not possessions simply an index of material wealth, telling us nothing whatever about people's opinions or their deeper values?

But there is another way of looking at it. When Mr Jones down the road suddenly appears behind the wheel of a high-powered sports car, he may first of all be declaring loud and clear to the neighbours that he is a successful man with money to spare. But he is saying more than that too. For he has chosen to buy a smart car and not a new conservatory or a world cruise or an extra pension. He is telling us something about himself, perhaps that he is not quite the grey, middle-aged man he looks. There is blood in his veins and fire in his belly yet, and maybe an eye for the girls too.

Messages like this are contained in every purchase which is in any sense discretionary and even in those that are simply satisfying a basic need like food or drink or shelter. Buying things is a form of expression which may reveal more about our values than we imagine. When we look at how a society spends its money and what importance it attaches to its purchases we discover something more than the sort of eccentricity that inspires Mr Jones to splash out on fast cars. We will learn about that whole society's priorities and values.

With this purpose in mind, we chose a list of ten things we knew from consumer surveys were owned by a great many people. We showed the list to our respondents and asked them a number of questions aimed at discovering their attitudes towards each item.

Here is our list: video recorder, colour television, microwave oven, car, stocks and shares, a holiday abroad for at least a fortnight a year, compact disc player, owning your own home, telephone, dishwasher.

You might want to argue with our choice. Why not a hi-fi instead of a compact disc player? Or a clotheswasher instead of a dishwasher? Fair points. But any list of ten is bound to involve selection. Our purpose was to choose a reasonable mix of goods and services, the fairly new (video recorder) with the relatively old (telephone), material objects like cars with other forms of possession or purchase like shares and holidays.

Our list immediately passed one important test. The items on it were indeed widely available to those who wanted them. The fact that people owned some things and not others was largely because that was their choice. Lack of purchasing power was not the major reason why people did not possess any of the items on our list. At most only around one person in four (29%) gave not being able to afford an item as the reason for not having it.

The next thing we wanted to establish was how many people possessed each of the things on our list. When we knew that, we could begin to assess people's attitudes to their possessions in terms of their priorities and preferences. Overleaf is our list a second time, now in order of the numbers who possessed each item.

We obtained these totals by adding together the answers to two questions. People were asked which of our items they 'have and couldn't do without' and which they 'have and could do without'. To get the other side of their preferences we also asked which they 'don't have but don't want' and which they 'don't have and can't afford'. The answers made it possible for us to do more than tell how widespread the ownership of each of the things on our list was. It enabled us to analyse how highly each of them was valued too.

The response to the very first item on the list, ownership of a colour television, immediately showed the paradoxical nature of people's attitudes to their possessions. Only 2% of people said they couldn't afford a colour television and another 2% said they didn't

15-1 What We Possess - Or Not

Q For each thing I read out, could you please tell me whether it is something
   you have and couldn't do without or something you have and could do without?

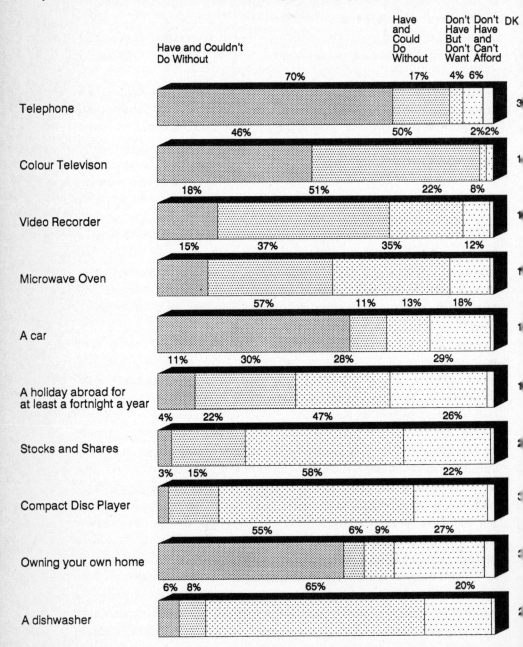

Source: MO

want one. With 96% owning colour sets, that makes colour television about as widespread throughout the population as it is possible for anything to be which is not either compulsory or an absolute necessity of life.

We were not surprised at television's prevalence because we had already discovered how vital the small screen was as a source for people's opinions and entertainment. What did surprise us was the take-it-or-leave-it attitude people felt towards this near-universal possession. More people actually said they could do without their colour televisions than said they could not. Only 46% said they could not do without, against 50% who said they could. In fact colour televisions were almost at the top of our list of items when we asked people which things they had but could do without. Old and working-class people valued their televisions most. But in the population as a whole, only video recorders were seen to be even easier to dispense with.

Video recorders are themselves now widely owned. Indeed Britain has more VCRs per head than any other country in the world. For every three people who have television sets, two have video recorders as well. But VCRs were seen as even more dispensable than colour televisions. Out of every seven people who owned a video, no fewer than five said they could do without it. More men (21%) valued them than women (15%) and more young (23%) than old (11%). Almost half the over 55s (47%) neither had them nor wanted them. But the feeling that videos were very much optional extras was common throughout the population.

The exact opposite was the case with the second most widely owned item on our list after colour television, the telephone. Almost nine people in ten (87%) now have one and most of those people valued their phones highly. The telephone was the item on our list which most said they couldn't do without. Of every nine people who had one, seven said they couldn't do without it. More women (73%) felt like that than men (66%), more old people (75%) than young (64%) and more middle-class (79%) than working-class (71%). Few people (4%) said they didn't want a telephone and slightly more (6%) said they couldn't afford one (among the 15 to 34-year-olds that figure rose to 11%). But the telephone emerges as unchallengeably the possession most widely felt to be indispensable. Yet two decades ago half of households had no telephone and one decade ago three households in ten were still without one. The telephone habit has grown fast and quickly struck strong roots.

Most widely valued the telephone may be, but not the most deeply. That distinction must fall to home ownership. Fewer people own their own homes than have telephones (61% against 87%) but those who do own their homes value the fact of possession very highly. When we asked which of the things on our list people had but felt they could do without, home ownership came firmly at the bottom. Only 6% of people agreed. Only one person in ten (9%), most of them council house tenants, said they neither owned their own homes nor wanted to; while 27% of people who did not own their homes gave not being able to afford to do so as the reason. It seems safe to say that home ownership is the thing most people want to hang onto if they've already got it and for which there is the greatest pent-up appetite among those who don't.

Cars run home ownership close in the indispensability stakes. Similar proportions of our respondents thought they couldn't do without their cars (57%) as couldn't do without owning their homes (55%). But since more people actually owned cars than homes (69% against 61%), more thought they could do without them (11% against 6%), more didn't have and didn't want cars (13% against 9%) and fewer said they couldn't afford them (18% against 27%), then cars clearly do not have the same grip on people's desire for possession as homes.

Not being able to afford something need not necessarily spell deep frustration. That certainly seems to be the case with holidays abroad. This was the thing the highest proportion of people (29%) said they could not afford. But then it was also one of the things people who did have them seemed able to do without most easily. No fewer than three in every four people who take at least a fortnight's holiday abroad each year thought they could do without their trips. Only 11% thought they couldn't do without while almost three people in ten (28%) neither had holidays abroad nor wanted to have them. Even though 42% of people are used to taking fortnight-long holidays outside Britain, the experience is evidently one a great many of them could give up without too much pain. If the 29% of people who told us they couldn't afford to travel really do feel frustrated, they should take comfort. To judge by the feelings of those who can afford it, they may not be missing so much after all.

If holidaying abroad is not seen as a passionate necessity, owning stocks and shares is seen to be even less of one.

There has been a surge of share ownership in the 1980s so that close to one-quarter of the adult population (26%) now have some at least. Among the items on our ownership list shares may have rated only the seventh most common possession out of ten. But compared with a decade ago, share ownership, boosted by successive privatizations, has rocketed. In 1979, when Mrs Thatcher took office, only one million people owned shares. By 1989 nine million did.

The share-owning habit has not, however, become anything approaching a strongly felt need. Only 4% of people told us they couldn't do without shares while almost half the population (47%) didn't even want them. Among Labour supporters, that figure was higher, though at 54%, not much above the average. Even among those who did have shares their possession was hardly seen as vital. No fewer than 85% of shareowners thought they could do without them, while only 15% thought they could not.

The remaining three items on our list are classic consumer durables – gadgets which make life easier or more entertaining. They are the microwave oven, the CD player and the dishwasher. Ownership of microwaves has spread to more than half the population (52%). But nearly four out of five people who had them thought they could do without them (37%), while the great majority of those who did not have them (35%) did not want them. High levels of indifference were also shown towards CD players and dishwashers. Dishwashers came top of our list of things people neither had nor wanted, and CD players came second.

People are apt to say they can't afford these things, even though they do not say the same about colour televisions or video recorders or cars, which are equally or more expensive. It looks as though saying you can't afford an item is often just another way of saying you don't care enough to want to spend money on it.

What does all this tell us about British attitudes to the affluence in which most of them live and which leaves them a large slice of their incomes to spend as they please? Does it make today's Britain, as is so often mournfully said, a wholly materialist society? The easy and fashionably cynical answer would be yes. But our survey indicates a state of mind less crude or crass than the label 'materialist' usually suggests.

People certainly like to own the products of the consumer society. They enjoy splashing out on video recorders, cars and holidays. But their priorities are eminently down to earth and practical. What they want to have and hang on to are the near essentials in today's world – telephones, cars and homes. Most of the others, from colour televisions to holidays abroad, they can do without and they know this very well.

Campaigns to change their minds are only likely to be successful if people are ready to have their minds changed. The Thatcher Government has tried to turn Britain into both a home-owning and a shareholding society and in both it can be said to have succeeded. But there is a difference between the two. A majority of people in Britain already owned their homes before Mrs Thatcher came to power. So the habit of home-owning was already well established before the sale of council houses at a discount boosted the home-owning majority.

Share-owning has shown a far more dramatic increase. Around eight times as many people owned shares in the late 1980s as ten years earlier. But it is far from having become a habit, let alone a priority or an essential like home ownership. That was made absolutely clear by our responses, which showed that only 4% of people could not do without their shares, compared with the 55% who would not willingly give up owning their homes.

The British, we conclude, are not the people to be rushed into making a necessity out of a pleasurable option. Their priorities in possession correspond closely with the economic and social realities of their time and place. They will happily join in the latest fashion for VCRs or shares, but they don't set overmuch store by them. When it comes to the pinch, a majority will even give up the television set on which they rely so heavily for their information and entertainment.

If this is materialism, then it wears a very sensible face.

16

British Activism

'THE COUNTRY – IT'S ALL CONTROLLED BY POLITICS,
REALLY. THE LABOUR PARTY HAS GOT ONE PART, THE
CONSERVATIVES GOT ONE PART.'

The British do not like to get involved. Commitment is not their thing. A kind of fatalism prevails.

From all we have learned about their myriad worries – from crime to drugs to pollution – and about their political scepticism – their lack of faith in Thatcherism, matched by their lack of conviction in any alternative – you might think we had discovered a gap which the citizen could plunge into and fill by becoming active on his own behalf.

But that is not the British way. They will take small private actions to express their worries or protect their interests, but most shy away from any more direct action or involvement.

Our survey gave us insights into this attitude from several angles but from whichever direction we looked the pattern was always the same. Worry though they may, the British are content to leave activism to a small minority of people.

We first came across this attitude when we were examining people's feelings about the environment. When we asked which of a list of ten things people had done in the previous year or two we quickly discovered that the most common pursuits were private and undemonstrative while the most uncommon were public and active.

Opposite is our list and the public's response to it.

From these answers it is clear that people do enjoy the natural world and are genuinely concerned about its problems. But many more preferred expressing their enjoyment than wished to turn their

16-1   Environmental Activism

Q   Which, if any, of the following things would you say you have done in the
last year or two?

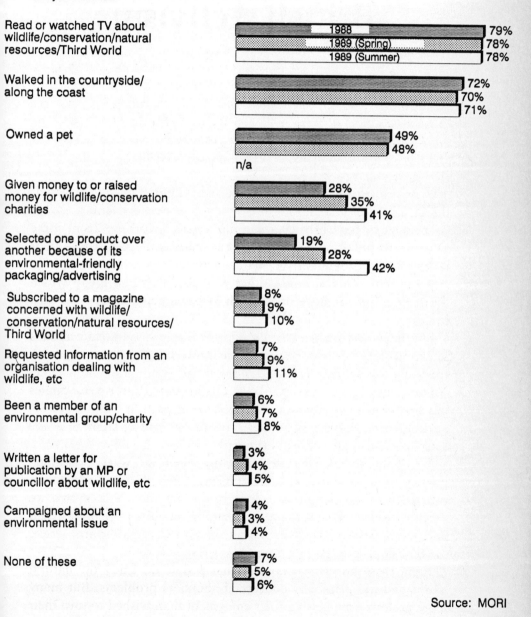

Read or watched TV about
wildlife/conservation/natural
resources/Third World
- 1988 — 79%
- 1989 (Spring) — 78%
- 1989 (Summer) — 78%

Walked in the countryside/
along the coast
- 72%
- 70%
- 71%

Owned a pet
- 49%
- 48%
- n/a

Given money to or raised
money for wildlife/conservation
charities
- 28%
- 35%
- 41%

Selected one product over
another because of its
environmental-friendly
packaging/advertising
- 19%
- 28%
- 42%

Subscribed to a magazine
concerned with wildlife/
conservation/natural resources/
Third World
- 8%
- 9%
- 10%

Requested information from an
organisation dealing with
wildlife, etc
- 7%
- 9%
- 11%

Been a member of an
environmental group/charity
- 6%
- 7%
- 8%

Written a letter for
publication by an MP or
councillor about wildlife, etc
- 3%
- 4%
- 5%

Campaigned about an
environmental issue
- 4%
- 3%
- 4%

None of these
- 7%
- 5%
- 6%

Source: MORI

concern into action. What they most liked to do was read or watch television programmes about environmental issues or walk in the countryside or along the coast. Just over three out of four did the first and just under three in four the second, making these the only two things on our list that a majority of people had actually done.

The next most popular activity was owning a pet. Almost half the population (48%) had done that – a very direct way of expressing pleasure in nature, perhaps, but a very private, family-centred way too.

Then we found that one person in three had given money to a wildlife or conservation charity and nearly as many had become sensitive enough to green issues to choose a product because of its advertising or formulation. Both these activities had also shown a significant jump in a single year, the only two items in our list to have done so. In 1988, when the same list was put to respondents, 19% said they had selected a product because of its environment-friendly packaging or advertising. A year later the number had moved up to 28% and in an even more recent survey it had moved up more sharply still to 42%. The earlier survey showed that 28% had given money to wildlife charities, while by early 1989 the number had risen to 35% and more recently still to 41%. These are striking demonstrations of the speed with which green concerns have been invading public attitudes.

All those things which attracted a third or more of people were either pleasurable in themselves or required no great exertion. It takes little effort to watch a television programme and not much more to drop a few coins in a charity collection box. The other items on our list did call for more active participation, as a consequence of which none attracted even one person in ten. To subscribe to a magazine with an environmental focus or write a letter to an MP or a local councillor, for instance, does require at least some energy and thought. But only 9% were willing to do the first and only 4% the second.

The same pattern emerged when we turned to consumer issues. Again, we asked people to tell us which from a list, this time of seventeen things, they had done in the previous year. Each item on the list represented a form of consumer response to making a purchase, ranging from simply looking at a label to organizing a boycott. This was our list:

16-2 Consumer Activism

Q Which, if any, of the following have you done in the last year?

Checked the sell-by date before
buying an item of food — 77%

Looked at the price of a product in
several shops before buying a brand — 48% (1979, 67%)

Checked food on sale for additives, artificial
colouring or flavouring or preservatives — 42%

Read or looked at "Which?" magazine
at least once — 21%

Complained verbally to a shop about the
quality of a product bought — 18%

Urged someone else to boycott a
brand of goods or manufacturer's goods — 9%

Complained verbally to the manufacturer
about the quality of a product bought — 9%

Complained verbally to a Citizens Advice
Bureau or independent ombudsman about
the quality of a product or service — 6%

Complained in writing to a shop about
the quality of a product bought — 6%

Complained in writing to the manufacturer
about the quality of a product bought — 5%

Taken legal advice or sued someone
about a purchase — 5%

Complained in writing to a CAB
or ombudsman about the quality of a
product or service — 3%

Been to a meeting of a group that looks
after customers' interests — 2%

Taken part in a demonstration or
boycott against a business, country
or manufacturer — 2%

Complained verbally to a Weights
and Measures Inspector — 1%

Joined the Consumers' Association
or other consumers' group — 1%

Complained in writing to a W&M Inspector — 1%

None of these things — 12%

Source: MORI

167

As with the environment questions, the easier and more passive forms of action were by far the most commonly undertaken. We found that 77% of people had checked the sell-by date on a food item; 48% had looked at the price of a product in several shops before buying (though interestingly that was many fewer than the 67% who had done the same when the identical question was asked in another survey ten years earlier: affluence and a lower inflation rate seem to have made the British much less willing to take the trouble to shop around); and 42% had checked food on sale for additives. A further one person in five (21%) said they had read or looked at *Which?* magazine at least once.

What all these have in common is their relative passivity. None of them requires a person to do much more than pick something up off a shelf and look at it or read the label. Having done this, the person makes up their mind and moves quietly on. Not a word need be said, not a whisper of protest uttered.

The other items on the list were, by comparison at least, almost aggressive. They required people to open their mouths, to confront someone, to write a letter, or even go to a meeting. As a result, far fewer people were willing to do any of them.

The most frequent form of this kind of action was to make a verbal complaint in a shop. Almost one person in five (18%) had gone so far as to do that. Fewer than one person in ten did any of the other things on our list. Nine per cent, for instance, said they had urged another person to boycott a brand of goods, 6% had taken the trouble to write to a shop to complain about something they had bought, 2% had been to a consumer group meeting, and another 2% had taken part in a demonstration or boycott.

As the amount of effort and commitment involved in each item increased, so the number of people willing to do it decreased. It should therefore come as no surprise to learn that one of the most popular forms of consumer response was to do nothing at all. When we asked people which of the things on our list of seventeen they had done, we built into the question the phrase 'if any', in effect asking them to say if they had done none of those things. And that was exactly what 12% of our sample said they had done – absolutely nothing. This ranked total inaction at sixth place in our hierarchy of consumer behaviour, 6% behind complaining verbally to a shop and 3% ahead of urging someone else to boycott a brand of goods!

Those two questions revealed the extent of people's readiness to act in their own interests in the two areas of the environment and consumer protection. Our third question took the issue of activism close to the heart of the matter, to the arena of political action itself.

But here, too, the pattern turned out to be the same. The easier, the more uninvolving the action, the more people were likely to take it. What was more, willingness to act turned out to be on the slide. We were able to make comparisons with ten years earlier on this question too and for the most part we found fewer people ready to participate in 1989 than there had been in 1979.

As with our two previous questions, we showed people a list and asked them which of ten things they had done in the previous two or three years. The list is opposite.

It was at least mildly reassuring for the health of British democracy to find that voting in general elections remained a fairly popular activity – in fact, the most popular political activity of all. More than two people in three, 68%, said they had voted at the last election (less than the actual turnout figure for the 1987 election, but our fieldwork was done a year and a half later).

Voting also stood out as being the only thing on our list which more than half our respondents said they had done. Indeed as few as one person in three (31%) had done the second most popular thing on our list, which was to help with fund-raising drives.

There was another big fall in numbers from the second to the third item, which was urging someone outside one's own family to vote. Hardly one person in five (18%) recalled taking the trouble to do even that, though this may reflect the generally lower level of interest in local elections and fading memories of the last general election.

When we reached the items which involved something like active participation, we were once again almost down to one person in ten in the population. Thirteen per cent of people told us they had presented their views to a local councillor or MP and the same percentage had either made a speech before an organized group or been elected the officer of an organization or club. (Trade union officer may well be what a large proportion of our respondents meant when they said 'yes' to that last question, since almost twice as many of the 23% of trade unionists in our sample said they were elected officers of an organization or club as did non-union members, i.e., one

16-3   Socio-Political Activism

Q   May I ask which of the things on this list you have done in the last two or
     three years?

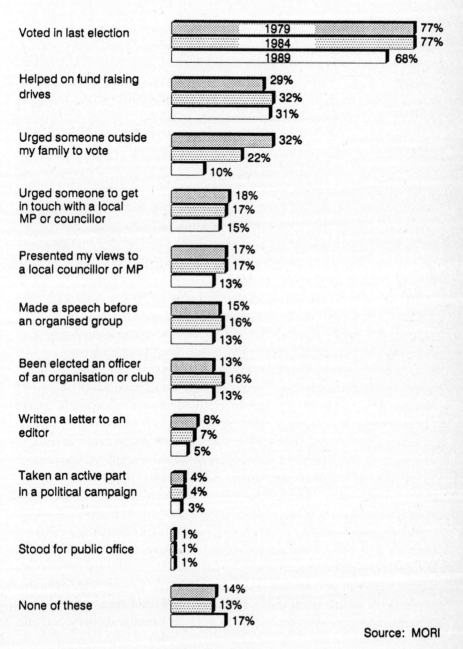

Voted in last election	1979	77%
	1984	77%
	1989	68%
Helped on fund raising drives		29%
		32%
		31%
Urged someone outside my family to vote		32%
		22%
		10%
Urged someone to get in touch with a local MP or councillor		18%
		17%
		15%
Presented my views to a local councillor or MP		17%
		17%
		13%
Made a speech before an organised group		15%
		16%
		13%
Been elected an officer of an organisation or club		13%
		16%
		13%
Written a letter to an editor		8%
		7%
		5%
Taken an active part in a political campaign		4%
		4%
		3%
Stood for public office		1%
		1%
		1%
None of these		14%
		13%
		17%

Source: MORI

171

in five of trade unionists against one in ten of non-trade unionists.)

No more than one person in twenty had done any of the last three things on our list. Five per cent had written a letter to an editor, 3% had taken an active part in a political campaign, and a bare 1% had stood for public office.

Apart from voting, then, all forms of political activity rate as no more than a minority pastime. Enthusiastic participation in politics is even more so. Only 6% of our sample said they had done five or more of the things on our list and 2% had done seven or more. The person who tells his elected representative his views is three times more likely to write a letter to an editor than the average. Someone who gets elected the officer of a club is three times more likely than the average to help on fund-raising drives, and so on. The minority who do get active seem determined to make up for the indifference of the majority who don't.

But not only are levels of participation low, for the most part they have been dropping. Compared with ten years earlier, involvement has at best risen only marginally but more often stood still and in most cases fallen. As our table shows, in 1979, 32% said they had urged someone outside their family to vote, against 18%; 17% had presented their views, against 13%; 18% had urged someone to get in touch with their local councillor or MP, against 15%.

After all this it will again come as no surprise to discover the popularity of the missing item on our list – doing nothing. This time round that was even more popular. It came fourth. Seventeen per cent of people had undertaken no political action whatever, as opposed to 14% in 1979.

It may be that one side-effect of the Thatcher decade has been to reduce people's belief in the value of political activity of any kind. Perhaps just by being there for so long, she has mesmerized the nation into believing that she is as unmoveable a part of the political landscape as Big Ben or the Transport and General Workers Union, and that there is nothing worth doing that will make any difference to that overwhelming fact.

Just as we found considerable consistency in activity levels among the population as a whole, whether on narrower issues like the environment or the broader issue of politics, so we found similar consistencies among sections of the population.

Middle-class people, for instance, are regularly more active than working-class. One in four of DEs (25%) and 15% of the C2 skilled working class did none of the things on our political activism list against only one in ten (12%) of ABs. Even when it came to checking prices in the shops, working-class people, who are on average worse off, were less likely to shop around for best buys than middle-class people, who are normally better off. On only one item could working-class people be said to be more active – they were more likely to own pets.

Younger and older people were also less likely to be active than the 35–54 age group which showed consistently higher rates of participation, especially in consumer questions like checking sell-by dates and additives. Exceptions were voting, where the over 55s were the keenest to turn out (81% said they had voted at the last election against 68% of people as a whole), and selecting products for their environmental-friendly packaging or formulation, where the under 35s scored well ahead of their elders.

Sex differences were not sharp or very surprising. Men were more likely to be politically active than women on most counts except fund-raising. Women were more sensitive to environmental-friendly packaging or formulation and to sell-by dates and food additives. But that may only be because they do more of the shopping. That may also explain why, on consumer issues, men were twice as likely to say they had done nothing at all (16% against 8%).

Tory supporters were marginally more active on most issues than Labour, though they lagged somewhat behind Labour supporters when it came to demonstrations and boycotts, no doubt because these forms of action are a long-established part of the Labour tradition while not being at all the Tory style.

In politics, the typical Tory supporter is a little more likely than the typical Labourite to make a speech, get elected to office in a club or help in fund-raising. The typical Labour supporter is a little more likely to urge people to vote, to get in touch with a councillor or take an active part in a political campaign.

From all this, enthusiasts for political and social action may conclude that the rest of the British are no better than a flock of sheep, content to be led by anybody who can be bothered to get involved.

But there is another way of looking at the evidence. What can seem to be indifference may just as well be a sign of maturity. Their unwillingness to stir themselves on political or social issues may be proof of a deeper confidence in their institutions than the British will easily admit, even to themselves. Is it not in politically turbulent countries that involvement is inescapable? In peaceful Britain, why bother? Action can be left to the busybody minority who care to take it. The British may be politically inactive because that is a luxury they instinctively feel they can afford.

17

British Types

'THERE ARE TOO MANY FOREIGNERS IN BRITAIN. WHATEVER
NATIONALITY THEY ARE, THEY HAVE A CHIP ON THEIR
SHOULDERS.'

Britain, like every other country in the world, is rife with myths and
stereotypes. A whole identity can be assumed in a person because of
some chance characteristic. Take hair, for instance. Redheads are
said to be fiery. Blondes have a better sex life. Long hair goes with
an artistic temperament, cropped heads with an aggressive one. Bald
men are wise ... and so on. See somebody's hair and you can
persuade yourself you know all about them.

But is there any truth in these tales? Or are they just fantasies,
superstitions that get tacked on to people for no reason, except
perhaps a chance association whose origin has long been forgotten?
Maybe Aristotle was bald. So for evermore baldness is taken as proof
of high intelligence.

We decided to test out three types to see, through the special lens
of our survey, what, if anything, marked them out from the rest of
the British. The characteristics we chose to look at were star signs,
left-handedness, and Irishness.

Does the star sign you were born under, we wanted to know,
really make you different from people born under other signs? Does
being left-handed single you out from the majority of right-handed
people in any other way than, say, forcing you to buy a different set
of golf clubs? Does being Irish or having Irish parents or grandparents
set you somehow apart from the native British?

In each case we did find some differences. But in no case was the
difference one we would have predicted from the stereotype.

175

The Stars

The most obvious difference between star signs is that more were born under some than others. People divided up like this: Aries, Leo, Virgo, Scorpio, Sagittarius, and Capricorn each claimed 9% of the population. Taurus, Gemini, Cancer, and Pisces each claimed 8%. Aquarius had 7%, and Libra 6%. This, so far as we can see, proves nothing, except perhaps that sexual intercourse is less popular in cold January and February, and more in Spring's March and April, when Sagittarians and Capricorns are normally conceived.

Besides this, we did note some inexplicable curiosities – which on inspection turned out to be disappointingly trivial. For instance, 12% of quality newspaper readers were Virgos, but only 4% were Aquarians. Popular newspaper readers were spread much more evenly between star signs.

One trade union member in three (32%) was either an Aquarian (10%), a Sagittarian (12%) or born under Aries (10%). One in four of the people who owned their own homes outright was either a Scorpio or a Leo, but only one in twenty was an Aquarian. Fourteen per cent of those who rented their homes privately were Sagittarians. But only 4% were born under Cancer and another 4% under Virgo.

When it came to politics the stars had almost no influence on party preference. The only significant difference was among the minor parties. Twelve per cent of SLD support came from Leos, but only 4% from Sagittarians. No less than 13% of SDP support came from Librans, while only 2% came from Geminis.

From all of this we conclude that the star sign under which you were born makes no significant difference to the way you act or think – or at least no difference that could be picked up by the sensors of our survey, though perhaps an astrologer or a tea-leaf reader could tease something from our findings that we have missed.

Left-hand/Right-hand

Left-handed people are seen as awkward and clumsy and of doubtful sincerity, by the Oxford Dictionary if not by us! They are also sometimes thought of as highly talented, even geniuses. Leonardo da Vinci was left-handed, so is Paul McCartney. But the main distinction we found was quite different and, in both senses of the word, genuinely sinister.

We first had to find out how the population divided. This was the result: left-handed 11%, right-handed 84%, ambidextrous 4%.

As we expected, left-handers were a minority – one in ten in the population. Men were more likely to be left-handed than women (13% to 10%). Women were more likely to be right-handed (87% to 82%) but less likely to be ambidextrous (5% to 3%). Sixteen per cent of single people were left-handed but only 11% of marrieds and 5% of widowed, separated and divorced.

Middle-class people were less likely to be left-handed than working-class. Nine per cent of ABs were left-handed compared with 14% of C2s and 12% of DEs.

In politics, strangely enough, left-handedness does seem to imply a mild leftward inclination: 13% of trade unionists were left-handed

against 10% of non-trade unionists, while 13% of Labour supporters were left-handed against 11% of Tories. Left-handers were also more likely to be light television viewers and environmental activists too.

That more or less exhausts the list of left-handers' peculiarities. But it leaves the most interesting – and the most literally sinister – peculiarity, which was between young people and old. Eight per cent of the over 55s said they were left-handed, but almost twice as many (14%) of the 15 to 34-year-olds said the same.

Our first thought was that this must be the effect of fashion. In the past, young people were often told that being left-handed was a handicap in life which the wise child avoided. So they trained themselves to be right-handers in order to stay with the mainstream. Perhaps, we thought, in older generations there were many more natural left-handers than our figures revealed, simply because they had made the switch and now counted themselves as right-handed.

Another possibility was then suggested to us. It is that left-handers do not live so long as right-handers. This emerged first from an unexpected source, a survey of American baseball players published in *Nature*. Baseball records make a handy pool of evidence because baseball is one of those games in which every characteristic of the players is recorded in loving detail. (It is also, as it happens, a game in which left-handers have a natural advantage, batting as they do a step nearer to first base.)

The difference in age at death was small, though real. The mean age when left-handed baseball players died was 63.97, against 64.64 for right-handers: not enough to account for the difference shown by our survey. Childhood training still looked the best explanation.

Then another possibility occurred to us. It was that left-handers as a whole die younger than do left-handed baseball players on their own. We got swift confirmation that this may be so from another study, by Professor Stanley Coren of the University of British Columbia. He found in a survey of Canadian students that left-handers were 89% more likely to suffer serious accidents than right-handers – 85% more likely to have a car crash, 54% more likely to hurt themselves with tools, 49% more likely to suffer serious injury at home, 25% more likely to suffer work mishaps and 20% more likely to be injured playing sports. The world, he found – and especially the motor car – is set up for the benefit of the right-handed. Perhaps those who told left-handed children they should convert to right-handedness were doing them a favour after all.

Irish

Until quite recently, the Irish were frequently seen as aliens in Britain. As late as the 1960s, landladies advertising rooms to let lumped them in with Commonwealth immigrants and declared both equally unwelcome with the same brutally hostile notice in their windows, 'No Blacks or Irish Need Apply'.

Such discrimination may now have been banned by law, but stereotypes linger on all the same. The Irish in Britain are still thought of as hapless working-class exiles, in flight from rural poverty and miserably alone in the big city. You will have no trouble identifying Irishmen of this type any Sunday morning, uncomfortable in a blue suit, hovering uncertainly on the pavement as he fills in time between mass and the magic hour when the pubs open, in which, when he finally bursts through the door, he will very likely find himself being served by an equally sad and lonely exiled Irish woman.

Or at least you think when you see people like these that you are seeing the typical Irish immigrant, but this is nonsense. There are a great many Irish people in Britain and they are thoroughly integrated in British ways of life and thought.

When we asked our sample if they were Irish or had Irish parents or grandparents, 14% said they had (up from 11% a decade ago). So around one in seven British people are Irish by birth or have Irish blood in them no further than two generations back.

But as a group they only stood out in marginal ways. The stereotype would have them all working-class and left-wing, for instance, but in fact they are only slightly more likely to be trade unionists than not (16% to 13%) and slightly more likely to support Labour than the Tories (17% to 15%).

The Irish in Britain are also very far from being uniformly working-class. If anything, they show the opposite trend of class membership to the rest of the nation. The lower the class rating, the fewer are Irish, whereas the opposite is the case with the population as a whole. The Irish accounted for 15% of ABC1s, the rest of the population 83%; 14% of C2s were Irish, against 84% of the rest; and 12% of DEs, against 86%.

The Irish person of myth certainly does exist. But he is the exception and no more typical of the Irish in Britain than characters like the Blimp, the Sloane or the Yokel are typical representatives of the English.

17-1 Two Interesting Groups

British Public % 100 All		Left–Handedness (11%=100%)	Irishness (14%=100%)
48	Men	54	44
52	Women	46	56
37	15–34	46	37
29	35–54	32	32
33	55+	22	31
39	ABC1	30	44
31	C2	38	30
30	DE	32	26
36	North	35	34
25	Midlands	25	21
39	South	40	45
65	Married	65	61
20	Single	28	19
15	Widowed/divorced	7	20
33	Child in h/h	36	33
16	Quality Reader	18	16
57	Popular Reader	60	55
29	None	27	29
29	Heavy TV	24	31
42	Medium TV	40	42
29	Light TV	36	27
38	Conservative	36	39
27	Labour	32	35
7	SLD	7	6
7	SDP	7	4
34	Thatcherists	37	30
54	Socialists	55	58

18

Britain in Perspective

The pattern of colour seen through the lens of a kaleidoscope can be changed by a flick of the hand. With the same swift magic we can put an entirely new perspective on the myriad items of information collected in our survey by running them through our computer using a completely different programme. That is what we have done to give you one last – but quite new – look at our findings.

The way we have presented our information so far has been essentially two-dimensional. Like a crossword puzzle, we have read people's opinions and attitudes across by their age, sex and so forth, and down by their strength of feeling on the issues we put before them. To put it another way, it is as though we have been looking at a snapshot of an apartment block containing all our 1,458 respondents, peering in at them one window at a time, able only to see what each successive window revealed to us as we went along.

But now, using a computer technique known as principal component analysis, we can take in the whole content of the building at a glance, as though we had suddenly acquired X-ray eyes. It is still a snapshot, not a movie, because what we see are people's attitudes at the moment of our survey, not as they may have evolved before or since. But now we can see how all our respondents and all the 369 answers they gave us relate to each other. We achieve something like three-dimensional vision.

To give a clearer idea of the technique, we will enlarge the apartment building analogy to one of a globe. A globe can be sliced into an infinite number of planes. On one such plane, let us imagine, we dot each of our respondents and cluster each by their principal characteristics, their age, sex and so on. On other planes, let us further imagine, we dot the more than half million answers they gave to our questions. We call the first plane earth and the dots of information on the other planes become the sky above it, twinkling with an infinity of stars which make up the universe of our findings.

'Infinity' may seem a large word to use here, but it will pass as an allowable piece of graphic exaggeration. Our survey was a representative sample of the British public so it can be projected, within a tolerance level of around plus or minus 3%, to represent the attitudes of the 42 million or so British adults we did not interview, who would have given us similar answers if we had. The stars in our universe of findings can therefore be legitimately counted, if not as infinity, certainly in the billions.

Let us now return to earth. The descriptive modelling technique we use to chart the relationships is called 'perceptual mapping'. We have taken the *Agorametrie* model, first tested several years ago in surveys of French public opinion and here validated using British public attitude data.

We created our perceptual map by using the answers to some fifty of the agree/disagree statements we put to our respondents to make a 'sky' of British public attitudes. Against that we set our 'earth', that is, the plane of people's principal characteristics we mentioned above – the way they identify themselves by age, sex, etc.

The *Agorametrie* method next divides the sky on which all our information is dotted into quadrants, each of which can overlay the others. We can choose whatever labels we like for each quadrant, as we have done, but the broad result is the same, whether in France or now Britain. The first quadrant tends to position the system, the second to destabilize it, the third to set it towards a new equilibrium, and the fourth to preserve that new equilibrium.

The four Quadrants:

Traditionalists (upper-right quadrant): people holding traditional values, tending to be older, C of E, more middle-class (though not so well educated), homeowners, married, and moralists who back the values, rules, norms and stereotypes with which society attempts to solve its problems.

Egalitarians (upper left): people more concerned with questions of political equality and liberty, they earn their title by challenging present society and its values. Also called *Challengers*.

Adventurers (lower left): independent, younger people, better educated and including the classic left intellectuals who produce new ideas about how to deal with society's problems.

Pragmatists (lower right): concerned with material satisfaction, on the right or centre politically and who can be said to go along with the system in order to make the most of it.

Looking at the map of the sky produced this way, it may seem that the upper-right quadrant is thronged with stars like the Milky Way while the lower-left quadrant is something of an empty quarter. But it is just as full, though perhaps we should say it is full of anti-matter. The point is that for every opinion held by those in the Traditionalist quadrant, the opposite point of view is held by Adventurers, and the opposite of Egalitarian attitudes are found in the Pragmatists' quadrant. Traditionalists tend to favour stricter discipline for young people, the banning of certain books, stopping immigration, women staying at home, and identity cards for football spectators. Adventurers on balance tend to disagree with all these things. Egalitarians believe that British Telecom should not have been privatized, that trade unions are essential to protect workers' interests, that it is right for the State to provide full financial support for the unemployed and that taxes on the wealthy should be increased. Pragmatists disagree. Bear this in mind when looking at all four of our quadrants.

The most interesting way of looking at our quadrants is to see how the key characteristics of the British people – age, class, etc. – are distributed along axes that cross our 'earth'.

Look, for instance, at the chart describing attitudes according to age. You can draw a more or less straight line from the youngest (bottom left) to the oldest (top right), from the Adventurers to the Traditionalists, with two kinks in the line. Note that both are skewed towards the Egalitarian (leftward) quadrant, though for different reasons. The first kink is for the 60 to 64-year-olds, born between 1925 and 1929 and therefore youngsters during the depression years and of an age to have served in or vividly recall the Second World War. The second kink represents the 35 to 39-year-olds, whose teenage years were shaped by Vietnam, the Paris uprisings of 1968, flower power, Carnaby Street and Britain's Swinging Sixties. In both cases, experience in their formative, teenage years seems to have made its mark and, in groups or cohorts, moved them to the left.

Other key characteristics – like class, income and, though to a lesser extent, religion – follow a similar path from bottom left to top right. Political allegiance provides another clear example, with Labour supporters strongly identified in the tenth year of Mrs Thatcher's Government as Egalitarians or Challengers and Conservatives as Pragmatists. Supporters of the former Alliance parties cluster close to Labour in the Challenger quadrant while the Don't Knows, on the basis of their position on our map, are more or less equally split between Tory support and support for the Opposition parties.

Gender tilts the other way, with the bias, although not strong, from NW (Egalitarian) women to SE (Pragmatic) men; similarly, though less skewed and more a straight left-right, are the left-handed and those of Irish descent. On the bias, and tilted sharply, are the Egalitarian socialists opposite to the Pragmatic Thatcherists.

Class makes an interesting picture: whether tested by the class of the head of the household or the occupation of the respondent, a similar pattern emerges with Ds and C1s central, Es well into the Traditionalist sector as befits their age and C2s more Traditionalist than the middle-class C1s. The interesting groups are the As, professional people and senior executives, the bosses, highly Adventurist, while the middle managers who report to them are much more Pragmatist. The Goldthorpe social-class analysis shows a similar if not so discrete or well-defined pattern. It is of greater interest to note how activists of every persuasion, fall neatly into the Adventurer quadrant.

Newspaper readership follows roughly the path we might expect, with *Guardian* readers squarely on the left, but clustered closely by *Independent* readers. The *Mirror, Star, Sun, Express* and *Mail* form an upper-left to lower-right line (NW to SE) with readers of the *Daily Telegraph* firmly planted in the middle of the quadrant of self-satisfied Pragmatists.

Those Pragmatists are, it seems, the most satisfied with their standard of living, while the Challengers are the least satisfied. This correlates closely with the line representing the aspiring (i.e., upwardly mobile) middle class as the most Pragmatic group, while the least pragmatic and the most likely to be Challengers are the downwardly mobile working class.

We British

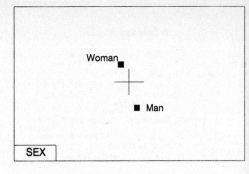

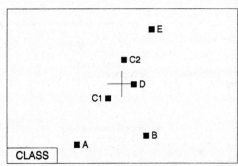

SEX

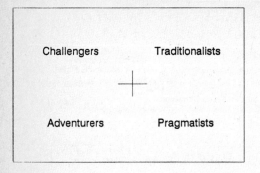

AGE

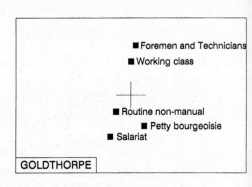

CLASS

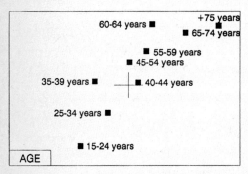

INCOME

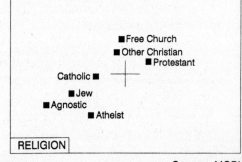

GOLDTHORPE

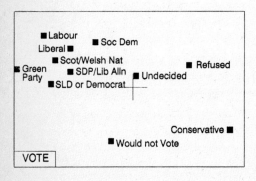

VOTE

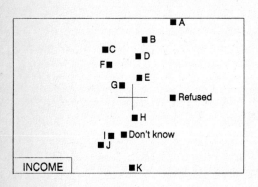

RELIGION

Source: MORI

18-1   The Agoramétrie Model of Britain - 1

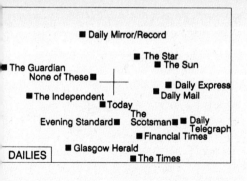

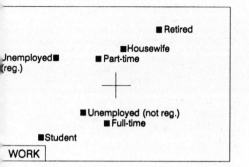

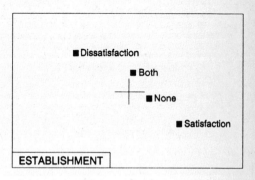

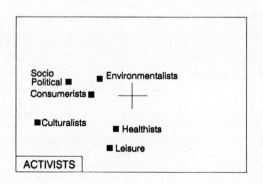

Source: MORI

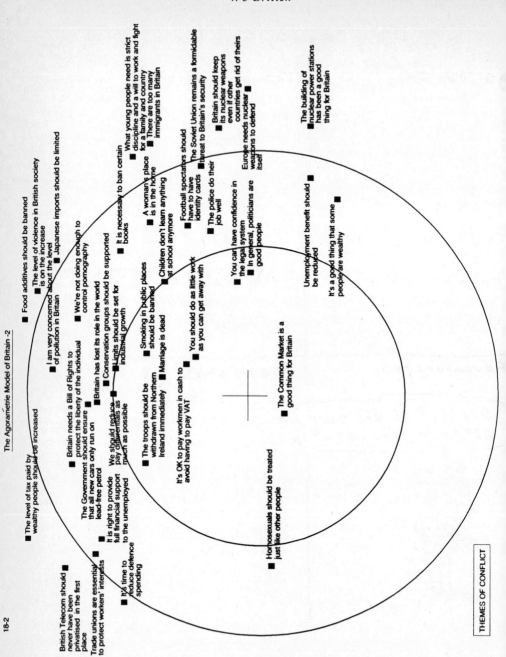

18-2

The Agoramétrie Model of Britain -2

The level of tax paid by wealthy people should be increased

Food additives should be banned

The level of violence in British society is on the increase

I am very concerned about the level of pollution in Britain

Japanese imports should be limited

Britain needs a Bill of Rights to protect the liberty of the individual

We're not doing enough to control pornography

The Government should ensure that all new cars only run on lead-free petrol

Britain has lost its role in the world

What young people need is strict discipline and a will to work and fight for a family and country

There are too many immigrants in Britain

It is right to provide full financial support to the unemployed

Conservation groups should be supported

Limits should be set for industrial growth

It is necessary to ban certain books

A woman's place is in the home

The Soviet Union remains a formidable threat to Britain's security

Britain should keep its nuclear weapons even if other countries get rid of theirs

The building of nuclear power stations has been a good thing for Britain

We should reduce pay differentials as much as possible

Smoking in public places should be banned

Children don't learn anything at school anymore

Football spectators should have to have identity cards

Europe needs nuclear weapons to defend itself

British Telecom should never have been privatised in the first place

The police do their job well

Trade unions are essential to protect workers' interests

The troops should be withdrawn from Northern Ireland immediately

Marriage is dead

You should do as little work as you can get away with

You can have confidence in the legal system

In general, politicians are good people

Unemployment benefit should be reduced

It's time to reduce defence spending

It's OK to pay workmen in cash to avoid having to pay VAT

The Common Market is a good thing for Britain

It's a good thing that some people are wealthy

Homosexuals should be treated just like other people

THEMES OF CONFLICT

Axis 2

alitarians   Traditionalists

                                          Axis 1

dventurers   Pragmatists

Well if that's your attitude, forget it!

A Last Word?

We would like to end with a definitive last word, on which you could close our book satisfied that you now know all that is worth knowing about British opinions, attitudes and values.

Unfortunately, however, opinion polling isn't like that. For one thing, it marries an art to a science, the art of asking questions to the science of sampling, to produce a hybrid creature which is always restlessly questioning itself and refining its techniques to produce more exact and truthful answers next time.

For another, a public opinion poll, no matter how large and comprehensive, is inevitably a snapshot, a picture of a mental landscape caught and frozen at one moment in time, whereas in reality opinion is always on the move. Sometimes change is so gradual that it could be caught only through a special sort of slow-speed camera, like the ones used by nature photographers to capture the unfolding of a flower. Sometimes it is much faster, almost needing a slow-motion camera to slow it down to an observable speed. Opinion can also move in complex and mysterious ways, apparently up-ending our understanding of ourselves almost overnight, as happened at those turning points of recent history like the General Election of 1979, the Falklands conflict of 1982, and the emergence of the Greens in 1989.

And who knows what is to come? We cannot tell, but we hope to be there to record it when it happens.

Appendices

1 'Activists' compared: table comparing the penetration and profile of the various attitudinal and psychographic groupings discussed in the text.
2 'Top line' results and precise question wording of the entire 'Living in Britain' survey questionnaire.
3 Social class definitions, as used by market research practice in Great Britain.

Appendix 1 <u>Activists</u>

<u>British Public</u> %		<u>Thatcherists</u> (34%=100%)	<u>Socialists</u> (54%=100%)	<u>Leisurists</u> (15%=100%)	<u>Socialise</u> (10%=100
100	All				
48	Men	55	44	55	49
52	Women	45	56	45	51
37	15–34	37	37	57	69
29	35–54	29	30	28	22
33	55+	34	33	15	9
39	ABC1	52	33	63	61
31	C2	27	33	27	28
30	DE	21	34	10	11
36	North	34	39	35	34
25	Midlands	24	25	18	20
39	South	42	36	47	46
65	Married	65	66	61	48
20	Single	21	19	30	46
15	Widowed/ divorced	14	15	9	6
33	Child in h/h	32	33	35	29
16	Quality Reader	22	13	31	30
57	Popular Reader	60	57	49	56
29	None	24	30	25	21
29	Heavy TV	25	33	10	10
42	Medium TV	43	40	42	43
29	Light TV	32	27	48	47
38	Conservative	65	23	42	43
27	Labour	11	41	19	22
7	SLD	6	8	8	5
7	SDP	3	9	8	5
34	Thatcherists	100	0	41	39
54	Socialists	0	100	53	56

Culturalists (12%=100%)	Socio-Politicalists (6%=100%)	Healthists (17%=100%)	Consumerists (14%=100%)	Environ-mentalists (16%=100%)
49	49	56	47	43
51	51	44	53	57
43	30	51	35	33
32	35	29	40	39
25	35	20	25	28
73	61	58	62	64
15	23	26	24	22
12	16	16	14	14
35	35	36	33	33
18	29	19	24	20
47	36	45	43	47
56	64	60	76	69
32	22	28	12	18
12	14	12	12	13
32	28	38	45	32
44	45	28	33	34
41	41	48	51	44
25	22	27	24	29
13	10	18	18	16
42	39	41	45	42
45	51	41	37	42
37	35	42	39	39
23	34	23	24	22
9	11	5	10	9
8	5	9	9	9
32	40	38	38	36
61	52	51	51	54

Appendix 2

Living in Britain

- EDITED, WEIGHTED DATA
- FIELD WORK 2-13 MARCH 89
- 1458 INTERVIEWS OVER 251 SAMPLING POINTS
- ALL DATA IN % TERMS
- * DENOTES < ½% BUT > 0%

- DATA BASED ON ALL RESPONDENT UNLESS STATED OTHERWISE
- ALL FIGS 1989 (UNLESS STATED OTHERWISE
- WHERE DATA DOES NOT ADD UP TO 100%, THIS IS DUE TO COMPUTER-ROUNDING OR MULTI-CODING

Sex of Respondent Base (1458)	19
Male.................... 48	
Female.................. 52	

Age of Respondent
15-24.................... 20	
25-34.................... 18	
35-39.................... 7	
40-44.................... 8	
45-54.................... 14	
55-59.................... 8	
60-64.................... 6	
65-74.................... 13	
75+..................... 6	

Respondent is %.	21
Head of household...... 54	
Not head of household.. 46	

Occupation of HEAD OF HOUSEHOLD
Position/Rank/Grade

....
Industry/Type of Firm

....
Quals/Degree/Apprenticeships

....
Number of Staff Responsible for

....

REMEMBER TO PROBE CWE/PENSION
Class (CODE FROM HOH OCCUPN ABOVE)
	%.	
A	3	
B	14	22
C1	22	
C2	31	
D	20	
E	10	

IF HOH WORKING: HOH Works in	23
Public sector	
Private sector	

Head of Household is	24
Self-employed............	
Not self-employed.......	

Working Status of HOH %.	
Full-time (30+hrs/wk+) .. 61	
Part-time (8-29 hrs) 4	
Not working (ie 8 hrs/week)	
- housewife 5	
- retired 20	
- unemployed (regist') . 3	
- unemployed (not regist' but looking for work 1	
- student 1	
- other 1	

RESPONDENT'S OWN OCCUPATION (IF NOT HOH)
Position/Rank/Grade

....
Industry/Type of Firm

....
Quals/Degree/Apprenticeships

....
Number of Staff Responsible For

....

Class (CODE FROM OWN OCCUPN ABOVE)	26
A	
B	
C1	
C2	
D	
E	

Working Status of Respondent ** %.	27
Full-time (30+hrs/wk)... 42	
Part-time (ie 8-29 hrs). 13	
Not working (ie < 8 hrs/week)	
- housewife 14	
- retired 17	
- unemployed (regist') . 4	
- unemployed (not regist' but looking for work 1	
- student 4	
- other 1	

na = 6%

RESPONDENT IF WORKING : Works in	28
Public sector	
Private sector	

RESPONDENT IF WORKING: is:	29
Self-employed	
Not self-employed	

** Based on all respondents whether Head of Household or not

Marital Status of Respondent Base (1483)   %   30
        Married 61
        Living with Partner
            (not married) 3
        Widowed.................. 10
        Divorced.............. 4
        Separated.............. 1
        Single 20

FOR OFFICE USE ONLY (CODE HOH)   %   31
        Salariat................. 22
        Routine non-manual...... 14
        Petty bourgeoisie 12
        Foremen and technicians. 10
        Working class.......... 37
        Other 7

Respondent is:
Trade union member 19   32
Not trade union member 76
no answer ——————————— 5

No. in household (incl. respondent)
Adults (aged 15+) 1 2 3 4 5 6 7 8 9+   33
Children (15) 0 1 2 3 4 5 6 7 8 9+   34

Ages of Children (in household)   %.

Aged 0-4 17
Aged 5-8 13   35
Aged 9-10 7
Aged 11-14 11
No children under 15........ 35

Home is: %.
Being bought on mortgage ... 46   36
Owned outright by household 22
Rented from Local Authority 24
Rented from private landlord 5
Other (WRITE IN & CODE '5') . 2
....

Length of Time in present home   %.
                                   37
0-1 year....................
Over 1-5 years..............
6-10 years..................
Over 10 years...............

Household Income (SHOWCARD GG)
Could you please give me the letter from
this card for the group in which you
would place your total household income
from all sources, before tax and other
deductions   %.   38
A 4
B 10
C 5
D 4
E 7
F 6
G 8
H 4
I 5
J 7
K 7
Refused 15
                                   39
Don't know 16

Daily Newspaper readership (SHOWCARD HH)
                                   %.   40
Daily Express 9
Daily Mail 10
Daily Mirror/Record 20
Glasgow Herald 1
Daily Telegraph 7
Financial Times 2
The Guardian 3
The Independent 4
The Scotsman 1
The Star 5
The Sun 22
The Times 3
                                   %.   41
The Evening Standard 2
Today 4
None of these 28

Sunday Newspaper Readership(SHOWCARD II)
                                   %.
News of the World 25
Sunday Express 11   42/
Sunday Mail (Scotland only)......... 6   43
Sunday Mirror 14
Sunday Post 7
Sunday Sport........................ 1
Sunday Telegraph 4
The Mail on Sunday 11
The Observer 5
The Sunday People 13
The Sunday Times 8
Scotland on Sunday 1

None of these 25

Share Ownership
Do you personally have shares in any
company?

IF YES: SHOWCARD JJ Which of these do
you have shares in? MULTICODE OK   %.
Yes, in the company I work for 2
Yes, in a company I used to
    work for 1   44
Yes, in a company a relative
    works for or used to work for ... 1
Yes, in a privatised company:
- British Telecom 6
- TSB 5
- British Gas 8
- British Airways 1
- British Steel 1
- British Aerospace .... *
- BP 1
- BAA 2
- Rolls-Royce 2
                                       45
- any other privatised company 2
Yes, in any other company 6
No 74
Don't know 1

QA How often do you watch television these days? Would it be nearer to 5 or more days, (PROBE: Do you view 5, 6 or 7 days) 3 or 4 days a week, 1 or 2 days a week or less often?

Box (1458) %. 46

Never	2
Less than 1 day a week	1
1 day a week	1
2 days a week	2
3 days a week	4
4 days a week	2
5 days a week	6
6 days a week	2
7 days a week	83

QB On a day when you do watch, for how many hours do you watch television?

%. 47

1 hour or less	5
Over 1, up to 2 hours	19
Over 2, up to 3 hours	24
Over 3, up to 4 hours	20
Over 4, up to 5 hours	15
Over 5, up to 6 hours	8
Over 6, up to 7 hours	4
Over 7, up to 8 hours	2
Over 8, up to 9 hours	1
Over 9 hours a day	2

ITV Area Normally Watched (SHOWCARD KK)

48

North East (Tyne Tees)	6
Lancashire (Granada)	12
Yorkshire	10
Midlands (Central)	15
Wales and West (Harlech or HTV) .	7
East Anglia (Anglia)	6
London	17
Southern (TVS)	11
South West (TSW)	3
Border TV	2
Grampian TV	1
Scottish TV	7

Respondent willing to be re-interviewed

%. 49

Yes	69
No	31

INTERVIEWER:

INTERVIEW STARTS HERE
ALL DEMOGRAPHIC QUESTIONS (EXCEPT THOSE NECESSARY TO CHECK THAT THE RESPONDENT FITS
YOUR QUOTA),MUST BE ASKED AT THE END OF THE INTERVIEW. NAME, ADDRESS AND TELEPHONE
NUMBER MAY BE ASKED AT THE BEGINNING OR THE END

Good Morning/Afternoon/Evening. My name is .... and I am conducting a MORI
poll about what kinds of things people think and do in Britain nowadays. Firstly
could I ask you..............

SKIP COL 50

Q1   What, if anything, do you consider good about living in Britain today?   PROBE:
      What else? What else?   %.   %.

OP 10
NSWERS
ase: All
(1458)

	%		%
• FREEDOM/CAN DO WHAT YOU LIKE	21	• THE PEOPLE	8
• LIKE LIVING IN BRIT/BEING BRIT	18	• WEATHER/CLIMATE	8
• FREEDOM OF SPEECH	17	• GREAT/BEAUTIFUL/	
• NATIONAL HEALTH SERVICE	13	GOOD COUNTRY	7
(• NOTHING	13)	• STANDARD OF LIV'	6
• COUNTRYSIDE	10	• GOOD EDUC/CHOICE OF EDUCATION	5

51-54

Q2   What, if anything, do you consider bad about living in Britain today?   PROBE:
      What else? What else?   %.   %.

SP 10
NSWERS
ase: All
(1458)

	%		%
• THE GOVT/GOVT POLICIES	14	(• NOTHING	10)
• UNEMPLOYMENT/LACK		• THE HEALTH SERVICE/	
OF JOB OPPORTUNITIES	12	UNDERFUNDING OF	8
• WEATHER/CLIMATE	12	• COST OF LIVING	8
• CRIME	11	• IMMIGRANTS/TOO MANY FOREIGNERS	8
• VIOLENCE	11	• TAXES/TAXMAN	7

55-58

Q3   How would you vote if there was a General Election tomorrow?
      (IF AGE 15-17 ADD: If you were old enough to vote?) CODE BELOW

      IF UNDECIDED OR REFUSED AT Q3
Q4   Which party are you most inclined to support?

                          Q3-5

ase: All
aving
arty
Q3-5
(1229)

Conservative........... ..	45
Labour...................	34
Social and Liberal Democrat	
(SLD or Democrat)	9
Soc Dem (SDP)..........	8
Liberal.................	
SDP/Lib Alln.............	
Scot/Welsh Nat..........	3
Green Party.............	1
Other...................	*
Would not vote..........	
Undecided...............	
Refused.................	

59/
60

Q5   If there was a candidate from the new merged Social & Liberal Democratic Party
     (Democrats or SLD) led by Paddy Ashdown, and from the Social Democratic Party (SDP)
     led by Dr Owen, which of these would you be most inclined to support?

     Conservative...........
     Labour.................
     Soc & Lib Dem
       (SLD or Democrat) .....   *SEE Q3/4*   61
     Soc Dem (SDP)...........
     Liberal................
     SDP/Lib Alln...........
     Scot/Welsh Nat.........
     Green Party............
     Other..................
     Would not vote.........
     Undecided..............
     Refused................

ASK IF PARTY CHOSEN AT Q3/4, IF NONE CHOSEN GO TO Q7a

Q6   How strongly do you support the . . . (PARTY CHOSEN AT Q3/4). Do you support it
     very strongly, fairly strongly, not very strongly or not at all strongly?

Base: All naming party
1986 = (2225)
1989 = (1229)

	1986				1989
	All	Con	Lab	Lib/SDP/All	
Very strongly	26	26	35	15	18
Fairly strongly	44	45	43	45	44
Not very strongly	24	23	18	30	27
Not at all strongly	5	5	3	8	8
Don't know	2	1	1	2	3

62

Q7a Do you think that the general economic condition of the country will improve, stay
     the same, or get worse over the next 12 months?

Base: All

	1985 (c.2000)	1986 (c.2000)	1987 (c.2000)	1988 (c.2000)	1989 (1458)
Improve	18	18	32	36	22
Stay the same	30	35	35	33	29
Get worse	44	40	25	24	45
Don't know	8	7	8	7	4

63

Q7b SHOWCARD A The things people can buy and do - their housing, furniture, food, cars,
     recreation and travel - make up their standard of living. How satisfied or
     disatisfied do you feel about your standard of living at present?

Base: All

	1988 (1030)	1989 (1458)
Very satisfied	16	18
Fairly satisfied	58	57
Neither satisfied nor dissatisfied	8*	8
Fairly dissatisfied	10	11
Very dissatisfied	8	6
Don't know/no opinion		*

64

* includes don't know/no opinion.

Base: AU (1458)

Q8 SHOWCARD B Here is a list of things some people have told us concern them, which would you say are the four or five that you would say concern you most?

ASK Q9 FOR EACH "CONCERNED" ABOUT AT Q8 OTHERS GO TO Q10

Q9 SHOWCARD C Now, looking at this card, for those you said concern yours. Could you please tell me which, if any, of the following are important, in influencing your thinking about them? (READ OUT THOSE CHOSEN AT Q8)

Q9 **

	(Q8) Con- cerned %	News- papers %	TV	Fri- ends	Fam- ily	Pol- iti- cians	The chu- rch	Teach- ers	Your Work	None of these	Don't know
a) AIDS	24	46	67	10	17	2	4	5	7	3	2
b) Britain's relationship with America	2	32	57	4	19	28	0	0	9	0	3
c) Common Market/EEC	8	41	46	4	9	29	5	3	11	8	12
d) Crime/law & order/ violence/vandalism	52	57	65	12	7	11	3	5	7	3	1
e) Defence/foreign affairs	3	36	57	1	2	43	5	2	7	7	0
f) Drug abuse	33	48	65	14	16	3	2	5	7	3	2
g) Economy/economic situation	8	45	40	10	13	37	4	4	10	3	2
h) Education/schools	25	24	25	18	35	15	3	41	10	4	3
i) Housing	17	30	24	22	31	20	1	1	10	5	3
j) Inflation/prices	25	44	47	8	22	19	1	1	8	6	6
k) Local government/ rate capping/ poll tax	18	45	42	11	15	38	*	1	7	5	2
l) Morality/ Permissiveness	9	44	53	17	23	5	25	8	5	3	1
m) National Health Service/hospitals	44	42	48	16	25	21	1	*	12	4	1
n) Northern Ireland	16	47	16	11	12	24	9	1	2	4	2
o) Nuclear power/ fuels	8	45	63	11	16	22	3	3	7	3	3
p) Nuclear weapons/ nuclear war/ disarmament	17	40	58	12	16	34	3	2	2	4	2
q) Pensions/social security	22	28	32	17	27	29	2	1	8	8	2
r) Pollution/ Environment	39	51	67	13	15	17	2	4	9	4	2
s) Pound/exchange- rate/value of pound	4	44	42	8	18	32	1	2	20	4	0
t) Privatisation	17	41	45	7	12	36	*	1	16	6	2
u) Race relations/ immigration/ immigrants	19	48	53	21	13	19	3	3	12	7	2
v) Taxation	15	27	29	9	22	29	1	0	26	3	4
w) Trade unions/ strikes	6	45	54	1	3	20	0	1	23	2	7
x) Unemployment/ factory closures lack of industry	26	49	47	23	17	24	1	1	16	3	2
y) Other (WRITE IN & CODE '1')	*	44	26	53	29	26	0	26	44	0	0
None of these	*										
Don't Know	*										

** based on all concerned about each issue at Q8

Q10 SHOWCARD D **Now looking at this list of of people and organisations, which, if any, would you say you are satisfied with in how it is performing its role in society? And which, if any, are you dissatisfied with in how it is performing its role in society?**
READ OUT/
ROTATE ORDER ASKED/ Base: All (1458)
TICK START┐

		Satisfied %	Dissatisfied %	
a)	The Church	49	22	
b)	Doctors	75	13	
c)	Trade Unions	28	42	
d)	The Police	64	22	
e)	Parliament	31	45	
f)	Civil Service	39	29	25/28
g)	The Royal Family	67	18	
h)	Major Companies	43	23	
i)	The Armed Forces	70	7	
j)	Teachers	48	30	
k)	The Legal System	34	43	
l)	National Newspapers	39	40	
m)	Government ministers	26	47	
n)	Universities	53	12	
o)	The Conservative Party	32	50	
p)	The Labour Party	24	52	
q)	The Centre Parties	20	46	
r)	The Nationalist Parties	11	53	
s)	The BBC	63	20	
t)	Independent Television	62	17	

Q11 SHOWCARD E **Which of the things on this card have you done in the past month?**

Q12 SHOWCARD E AGAIN **And which, if any, of these activities did you do more frequently in the last 12 months than you did, say 2-3 years ago?**

		Q11 1989 Base: All (1458) %	Q12 1984 (1901) %	1983 (1999) %	1982 (1458) %
a)	Competitive sport	16	6	6	6
b)	General exercise/keep fit	42	19	16	15
c)	Been to a wine bar(s)	12	4	3	2
d)	DIY	39	19	19	10
e)	Gardening	40	34	24	11
f)	Been out for a Sunday afternoon drive	39	12	10	6
g)	Been to pubs	46	16	13	9
h)	Been to the cinema	16	5	7	4
i)	Been to the theatre	15	6	5	4
j)	Watched TV/Video	89	39	29	21
k)	Had friends round to your home for a meal or drink	51	22	18	9
l)	Been to a nightclub/disco	15	9	6	4
m)	Been away for the weekend	23	13	12	6
n)	Been to a sports club	20	7	6	3
o)	Been to a social/working mens' club	15	n/a	n/a	3
p)	Been away on holiday	13	17	14	6
q)	Been to a restaurant	49	18	16	13
r)	Read a book	64	n/a	n/a	15
s)	Made your own beer or wine	6	n/a	n/a	2
t)	None of these	1	n/a	n/a	26
u)	Don't know	*	n/a	n/a	5

Q13 SHOWCARD F **Which, if any, of these have you been to in the past twelve months?**

Base: All

	1981 (974)	1985 (1090)	1988 (2022)	1989 (1458)
a) Art Exhibition	19	16	24	17
b) Pop concert	13	12	16	10
c) Library	52	52	54	49
d) Theatre	24	24	33	25
e) Opera	3	3	4	3
f) Classical ballet	4	3	4	2
g) Museum	29	25	40	27
h) Modern dance	18	10	15	8
i) Orchestral concert	10	9	12	10
j) Cinema	41	33	43	32
k) Pantomime	10	13	15	13
l) Football match	n/a	n/a	20	14
None	n/a	n/a	21	23
Don't know	n/a	n/c	n/c	*

Q14 SHOWCARD G **And which, if any, of the things on this list have you done in the past two days? Just read out the appropriate letter**

Base: All

	1985 (1029)	1989 (1458)	
a) Eaten fresh fruit	72	78	
b) Eaten wholemeal bread	51	50	
c) Eaten fresh green vegetables	78	80	
d) Eaten high fibre or wholemeal cereal	37	47	
e) Had sugar in tea or coffee	54	49	
f) Drunk a glass of whole milk	29	27	35/36
g) Had an alcoholic drink/beer/wine	46	50	
h) Had fish and chips or a fry-up	33	32	
i) Smoked a cigarette, pipe or cigar	37	34	
j) Taken part in a team sport (eg, football, cricket)	5	6	
k) Taken part in an individual sport or exercised (eg, swimming, jogging)	17	17	
l) Taken marijuana or other drugs	1	1	
m) Taken any medicine	28	32	
n) Been on a diet to lose weight	10	14	
o) Taken vitamin pills	10	17	
p) Taken aspirin	n/a	15	
None of these	*	1	

Q15 SHOWCARD H **And which if any of these things have you done in the past two months**

Base: All (1458)

a) Given up/cut down on eating eggs or chicken	23	37
b) Given up/cut down on eating soft cheeses	11	
c) Taken "the pill"	7	
None of these	68	

Q16 SHOWCARD hh **Which, if any, of the following things would you say you have done in the last year or two?** JUST READ OUT THE LETTER OR LETTERS *1988* *1989* 38

Base: All (1015) (1458)

a) Walked in the countryside/along the coast.................... 72 70
b) Read/Watched TV about wildlife/conservation/natural
   resources/Third World.. 79 78
c) Selected one product over another because of its
   environmental-friendly packaging/advertising................. 19 28
d) Been a member of an environmental group/charity
   (even if you joined more than two years ago).................. 6 7
e) Given money to or raised money for wildlife/conservation
   charities.. 28 34
f) Campaigned about an environmental issue....................... 4 3
g) Subscribed to a magazine concerned with
   wildlife/conservation/natural resources/Third world.......... 8 9
h) Written a letter for publication to an MP/councillor
   about wildlife/conservation/natural resources/Third World..... 3 4
i) Requested information from an organisation dealing
   with wildlife/conservation/natural resources/Third World...... 7 9
j) Owned a pet.. 49 49

Q17 SHOWCARD I **Which, if any, of the following have you done in the last year?** Just
read out the letter or letters.   Base: All (1458)**

a) Checked the sell-by date before buying an item of food............... 77
b) Complained verbally (ie face-to-face conversation or by
   telephone) to a Citizens Advice Bureau or independent
   ombudsman about the quality of a product or service which
   you have bought/received... 6
c) Complained in writing (ie by letter) to a Citizens Advice
   Bureau or independent ombudsman about the quality of a
   product or service which you have bought/received.................. 3
d) Complained verbally (ie face-to-face conversation or by
   telephone) to a shop about the quality of a product bought.......... 18
e) Complained in writing (ie by letter) to a shop about the
   quality of a product bought.. 6   39/
f) Complained verbally (ie face-to-face conversation or by   40
   telephone to the manufacturer about the quality of a product bought. 9
g) Complained in writing (ie by letter) to the manufacturer
   about the quality of a product bought.............................. 5
h) Checked food on sale for additives, artificial
   colouring, flavouring or preservatives............................. 42
i) Joined the Consumers' Association or other consumer group............. 1
j) Complained verbally (ie face-to-face conversation or by
   telephone) to a Weights and Measures Inspector...................... 1
k) Complained in writing (ie by letter) to a Weights and
   Measures Inspector... 1
l) Read or looked at "Which?" magazine at least once in the last year.... 21
m) Taken legal advice or sued someone about a purchase.................. 5
n) Taken part in a demonstration or boycott against a business,
   or a country, or a manufacturer and its goods 2
o) Been to a meeting of a group that looks after customers' interests ... 2 (3)
p) Looked at the price of a product in several shops before buying a brand 48 (67)
q) Urged someone else to boycott a brand of goods or manufacturers goods 9 (8)
   None of these... 12
   Don't know.. 0

** Figures in brackets = Base All 1979 (2010)

Q18 SHOWCARDS J - S People have
different views about the ideal
society. This card shows a number
of alternatives. Please read each
pair of statements and then tell
me which one, in each case, comes
closest to your ideal - statement
A or statement B. Which is
closest to your ideal for the
first pair of statements? REPEAT
FOR EACH PAIR OF STATEMENTS

SHOWCARD J
A. A mainly capitalist society in
    which private interests and   */.
    free enterprise are most
    important .... (43) 39   41
B. A mainly socialist society
    in which public interests
    and a more controlled
    economy are most important (49) 47

    No Opinion .... (8) 14

SHOWCARD K
A. A society which emphasises
    the social and collective
    provision of welfare ..... (55) 54   42
B. A society where the
    individual is encouraged
    to look after himself .... (40) 40

    No Opinion .... (5) 6

SHOWCARD L
A. A society which emphasises
    keeping people in jobs even
    where this is not very
    efficient .... (42) 42   43
B. A society which emphasises
    increasing efficiency
    rather than keeping people
    in jobs .... (50) 47

    No Opinion .... (8) 11

SHOWCARD M
A. A society which allows
    people to make and keep
    as much money as they can (53) 52   44
B. A society which emphasises
    similar incomes and rewards
    for everyone .... (43) 40

    No Opinion .... (4) 9

SHOWCARD N
A. A society in which the
    creation of wealth is
    more highly rewarded ... (16) 12   45
B. A society in which the
    caring for others is more (79) 81
    highly rewarded ....

    No Opinion .... (5) 7

SHOWCARD O
A. A country in which the
    schools provide children   '/.
    with a wide-ranging
    general education 61
B. A country in which the   [46]
    schools provide children
    with the particular
    skills and attitudes
    wanted by employers
    today 33

    No opinion 6

SHOWCARD P
A. A country which emphasises
    protection of the
    environment at the expense 75   [47]
    of economic growth ......
B. A country which emphasises
    economic growth at the
    expense of the environment 12

    No opinion 12

SHOWCARD Q
A. A country which has a signi-
    ficantly higher tax-rate
    for ordinary tax-payers,
    in order to pay for
    generous support for the   71   [48]
    elderly and the poor ....
B. A country which has a signi-
    ficantly lower tax rate
    for ordinary tax payers and
    provides only minimum
    support for the elderly
    and the poor 15

    No opinion 14

SHOWCARD R
A. A country which has signi-
    ficantly higher tax-rate
    for ordinary tax-payers   [49]
    and provides a sub-
    stantially better health
    service 78
B. A country which has a
    significantly lower tax-
    rate for ordinary
    taxpayers and provides
    only a minimum health
    service 11

    No opinion 11

SHOWCARD S
A. A country which has no
    nuclear weapons even if
    the United States and the   [50]
    Soviet Union still have
    theirs 52
B. A country which has nuclear
    weapons even if the United
    States and the Soviet
    Union have given up theirs 28

    No opinion 21

Base: All (1458), Figures in brackets = Base All 1988 (1030)

Q19   SHOWCARD T Here is a list of issues some people might think are immoral or morally wrong. Which of them, if any, do you personally think are morally wrong? Just read out the appropriate letter or letters.

_1988_   _1989_

Base: All (888) (1458)

		1988	1989
A	The use of hard drugs such as heroin	88	89
B	Soccer hooliganism	78	75
C	The use of soft drugs such as cannabis	66	60
D	Scenes of explicit violence on TV	54	53
E	Pornography in the cinema	51	47
F	Having sexual relationships with someone who is married to someone else	51	52
G	Scientific experiments on human embroyos	50	52
H	Scientific experiments on animals	49	50
I	Homosexual relationships between consenting adults	44	40
J	Full frontal male nudity on TV	40	39
K	Soft porn magazines in shops and newsagents	36	38
L	Strip shows	29	25
M	Having a child with a person you are not married to	23	24
N	Topless page 3 girls	22	21
O	Couples living together who are not married	14	13
P	Divorce	n/a	11
Q	Abortion	n/a	35
R	Euthanasia	n/a	22
S	Setting up sperm banks	n/a	16
T	Capital punishment	n/a	22
U	None of these	n/a	*
V	Don't know/no opinion	n/a	*

54/55

Q20   SHOWCARD U Now this is a list of things which some people think make for a successful marriage. Which of these if any do you think important in a successful marriage?

Base: All (1458)

a)	Faithfulness	86
b)	An adequate income	49
c)	Being of the same social background	20
e)	Mutual respect and appreciation	78
f)	Shared religious belief	20
g)	Good housing	46
h)	Agreement on politics	8
i)	Understanding and tolerance	79
j)	Living apart from your in-laws	41
k)	Happy sexual relationship	70
l)	Sharing household chores	58
m)	Children	48
n)	Tastes and interests in common	62
o)	Other (WRITE IN AND CODE "2")...................	
	....	1
p)	None of these...................................	*
q)	Don't know......................................	1

56/57

Q21   SHOWCARD V Here is a list of things which some people have said are the main
       contributing factors to divorce in Britain today. Which, if any, do you think
       are the main causes?   Base: All (1458)

       a) Poverty 56
       b) Poor housing...................................... 46
       c) Career pressures on men 26
       d) Women working/not at home with children 21
       e) Too high expectations of marriage 46   58/59
       f) Money/financial difficulties 70
       g) Sexual problems 43
       h) Being childless.................................. 15
       i) Having children 15
       j) Family/in-law problems 28
       k) Less social stigma for divorce 22
       l) Alcohol...56

       m) Drugs.. 50
       n) Lower religious standards........................ 13
           Other (WRITE IN AND CODE '3')..................... 1

       ....

       Don't know /none................................... 2

Q22   SHOWCARD W Here is another list, this time of crime, which of these, if any,
       would you consider to be very serious crimes?

                              Base: All (1458)

       a) Avoiding fares on public
          transport 9
       b) Sexual abuse of children 96
       c) Tax evasion 24
       d) Shop-lifting 23
       e) Financial swindles in the
          City of London 37
       f) Armed robbery 85
       g) Football hooliganism 52
       h) Mugging 81
       i) Rape 95   60/61
       j) Burglary 51
       k) Driving when over the legal
          limit of alcohol 78
       l) Drug-taking 58

       m) Claiming State Benefits to
          which you're not entitled 31
       m) Terrorism................................ 87
       o) Discrimination on the grounds
          of race or sex........................... 31

          None of these............................. 0
          Don't know................................ *

Q23 SHOWCARD X **On this card is a list of fears which some people may have. Which, if any, of them are fears which you personally have?** Just read out the letter or letters for any which apply.

Base: All (2078) (1458)

		1981	1982	
A	Going out at night alone	37	36	
B	Using public transport at night	19	24	62
C	Being attacked in my own home	29	41	
D	Being raped	26	41	
E	Being mugged (ie attempted or actual theft of my possession(s) while still on my person)	38	48	
F	Some other form of attack (other than C, D or E)	18	24	
G	Having one or more of my possessions stolen (not from my person)	24	21	
H	Having my home burgled	60	58	
I	Having my home or other possessions vandalised	49	48	
	Other (WRITE IN AND CODE O)			
	....	1	*	
	None of these	11	14	
	Don't know	2	*	

Q24 SHOWCARD Y **Which of the factors on this card are in your view the main causes of crime in Britain today?**

Base: All (1458)

a)	Too lenient sentencing	62
b)	Poverty	40
c)	Lack of discipline at school	51
d)	Lack of discipline from parents	75
e)	Television	27
f)	Drugs	71
g)	Alcohol	62
h)	Poor Policing	20
i)	Unemployment	62
j)	National Newspapers	10
	Other (WRITE IN AND CODE 'X')	
	....	1
	None of these	*
	Don't know	*

63/64

Q25 SHOWCARD Z **For each thing I read out, could you please tell me, using this card, whether it is something you have and couldn't do without, something you have and could do without, something you don't have but don't want, or something you don't have and can't afford?**

Base: All (1458)

READ OUT/TICK START	A Have and couldn't do without	B Have and could do without	C Don't have but don't want	D Don't have and can't afford	Don't know
a) Telephone	70	17	4	6	3
b) Colour Television	46	50	2	2	1
c) Video Recorder (VCR)	18	51	22	8	1
d) Microwave oven	15	37	35	12	1
e) A car	57	11	13	18	1
f) A holiday abroad for at least a fortnight a year	11	30	28	29	2
g) Stocks and shares	4	22	47	26	2
h) Compact Disc Player	3	15	58	22	3
i) Owning your own home	55	6	9	27	3
j) A dishwasher	6	8	65	20	2

Q26 Which of these – Europe, The Commonwealth, or America – is the most important to Britain?

	Base All: 1969 (c.1000)	1984 (c.1000)	1986 (c.1000)	1989 (1458)	
Europe	21	39	39	50	
Commonwealth	34	25	26	21	75
America	34	26	29	19	
Don't know	N/a.	N/a	N/a	10	

Q27 Which of the superpowers, if either, contributes the biggest threat to world peace in your view, the USA (the Americans) or the USSR (the Russians)?

	Base: All 1986 (1080)	1989 (1458)	
USA	20	26	
USSR	38	34	76
Both equally	34	28	
Neither	5	8	
Don't know	3	4	

Q28 SHOWCARD AA Using this card, could you tell me which statement best describes how often or not you visit a place of worship?

Base: All (1458)

I never attend	18	
I attend only for special occasions (eg marriage, birth, death) ...	43	
I occasionally attend	22	77
I regularly attend (ie at least once a fornight)	17	
Don't know	*	

Q29 Which, if any, of the things I'm going to read out do you believe in?

YES

READ OUT AND CODE ANSWER FOR EACH	Base: All 1957** (c.1500)	1985 ( )	1989 (1458)	
God	(41+37)	76	76	78
Life after death	54	45	49	79
			CARD ③ 9	
A soul	n/a	59	68	10
The Devil	34	30	37	11
Hell	n/a	27	31	12
Heaven	n/a	57	60	13
Sin	n/a	69	69	14
Astrology	n/a	n/a	37	15
Opinion polls	n/a.	n/a	56	16

** 1957 Group Q 'Which of these statements comes closest to your belief'

	%
• There is a personal god	41
• There is some sort of spirit/god or life force.	37
• I don't know what to think	16
• Don't really think there is any sort of spirit/god or life force.	6

Q30 SHOWCARD BB **What is your religious denomination?**

Base: All

	1985 (1231)	1989 (1458)
Roman Catholic	11	13
Church of England, Scotland, Wales or Ireland (Protestant)	68	65
Free church/non-conformist	6	7
Jew	N/a	1
Muslim	n/a	1
Hindu	N/a	*
Buddhist	N/a	*
None - Agnostic	N/a	4
- Atheist	N/a	4
Other Christian (WRITE IN AND CODE 'O')	n/a	5
....		
Other non-Christian (WRITE IN AND CODE 'X').	N/a	1

17

....

Q31 **Most people say they belong either to the middle-class or to the working class. If you had to make a choice, would you call yourself middle-class or working-class?**

Q32 **And which social class would you say your parents belonged to when you started at primary school?**

Base: All

	Q31 1986 (2569)	1989 (1458)	Q32 (1458)
Middle	28	30	21
Working	66	67	75
Don't know	5	4	4

18/19

Q33 SHOWCARD CC **And which class would you describe yourself as belonging to from this list?**

Q34 SHOWCARD CC AGAIN **And which class from this list would you say your parents belonged to when you started at primary school?**

Base: All (1458)

	Q33 %	Q34 % (1458)
Upwardly mobile middle-class	6	4
Stable middle-class	23	18
Downwardly mobile middle-class	4	2
Upwardly mobile working class	16	11
Stable working-class	42	56
Downwardly mobile working-class	3	4
Don't know	5	6

20/21

Q35 **I am going to read out some things that people have said about America and Americans. Please tell me whether on balance, you agree or disagree with each one?**

Base: All 1986 (1089), 1989 (1458)

	Agree %	Disagree %	Don't know %	
I like Americans as people	(66) 69	(16) 16	(18) 15	22
I would like to go on holiday to America	(64) 66	(34) 32	(2) 2	23
I think we can learn a great deal in this country from America	(46) 40	(44) 52	(10) 8	24
I would like to live in America if I could not live in Britain	(31) 23	(62) 73	(7) 4	25
We would be better off if we were more like the Americans in many respects	(22) 15	(67) 78	(11) 7	26

Q36 Could you please tell me if you are presently working (either full or part-time), or not?

Working (full or part-time) .... *N/a.*
Not working   27

Q37 ASK ONLY IF WORKING
Which of these statements comes nearest on the whole to what you think of your present (main) job?

Base: All working

	1976** (1038) %	1988 (1063) %	1989 (798) %
Very satisfied	32	30	34
Fairly satisfied	51	51	48
Neither satisfied nor dissatisfied	8	8	6
Fairly dissatisfied	} 8	7	8
Very dissatisfied		2	2
Don't know	N/a.	2	1

28

Q38 SHOWCARD DD Please indicate which of these statements comes closest to describing your views towards your current job?

Base (Company Aggregate)*** | 1989 (1458)

A   I'm not really interested in the company/organisation I work for it's just a job 9   10

B   I like to know what's going on in the company/organisation I work for, but I don't really want to get involved 26   20   29

C   I like to know what's going on in the company/organisation I work for and would like to become more involved 45   24

D   I like to know what's going on in the company/organisation I work for and am already involved 20   38

Don't know .... N/a.   7

Q39 ASK ALL
Generally, speaking, do you think of yourself as Conservative, Labour, Social & Liberal Democrat, SDP, or what?

Base: All (1458) %

Conservative.............	38
Labour..................	29
Soc & Lib Dem (SLD or Democrat)	5
Soc Dem (SDP).............	4
Liberal.................	1
SDP/Lib Alln.............	2
Scot/Welsh Nat...........	6
Green Party..............	1
Other....................	1
Would not vote...........	4
Undecided................	8
Refused.................	1

30

** 1976 Manual workers only.

*** Company (morel) Aggregate based on employee attitude surveys from a variety of companies *not* a national profile.

Q40 **Which Party did you vote for at the last General Election, in June 1987? If you are not sure, or did not vote, please say so.**

Base: All (1458)

Conservative.............	37
Labour....................	24
Liberal....................	5
SDP	5
Liberal/SDP Alliance	4
Scot/Welsh Nat...........	2
Green Party..............	*
Other.....................	*
Did not vote.............	15
Too young to vote	5
Can't remember	1
Refused..................	1

31

Q41 SHOWCARD EE **May I ask you which of the things on this list you have done in the last two or three years?**

Base: All

		1979 (2010)	1984 (2039)	1989 (1458)
a)	Presented my views to a local councillor or MP	17	17	13
b)	Written a letter to an editor	8	7	5
c)	Urged someone outside my family to vote	32	22	18
d)	Urged someone to get in touch with a local councillor or MP	18	17	15
e)	Made a speech before an organised group	15	16	13
f)	Been elected an officer of an organisation or club	13	16	13
g)	Stood for public office	1	1	1
h)	Taken an active part in a political campaign	4	4	3
i)	Helped on fund raising drives	29	32	31
j)	Voted in last election	77	77	68
	None of these	14	13	17

32

Q42 **Which television channel would you say you watch most, BBC1, BBC2, ITV, or Channel 4?**

Base: All (1458)

BBC1.......................	34
BBC2.......................	5
ITV........................	34
Channel 4..................	4
All Equally...............	25
Don't know................	2

33

Q43 SHOWCARD FF **What is your star sign?**

Base: All (1458)

Aries (Mar 21 - Apr 20).............	9
Taurus (Apr 21 - May 21)...........	8
Gemini (May 22 - June 21)..........	8
Cancer (June 22 - July 23).........	8
Leo (July 24 - Aug 23).............	9
Virgo (Aug 24 - Sept 23)...........	9
Libra (Sept 24 - Oct 23)..........	6
Scorpio (Oct 24 -Nov 22)..........	9
Sagittarius (Nov 23 - Dec 21)......	9
Capricorn (Dec 22 - Jan 20)........	9
Aquarius (Jan 21 - Feb 19).........	7
Pisces (Feb 20 - Mar 20)..........	8

34

Q44 **Are you primarily left or right-handed?**

%.

Primarily left-handed............	11
Primarily right-handed...........	84
Both equally/Ambidextrous........	4
Don't know......................	*

Base: All (1458)   35

Q45 **Are you, your parents, or your grandparents Irish?**   Base: All (1458)   35

Yes.............................	14
No..............................	84
Don't know......................	2

Q46 Finally, here is a list of statements some people have made. For each one would you please circle the number under the appropriate heading according to how strongly you agree or disagree with each statement. HAND RESPONDENT SELF-COMPLETION QUESTIONNAIRE.

Base : All (1458)

		Strongly agree %	Tend to agree %	Neither agree nor dis- agree %	Tend to disagree %	Strongly dis- agree %	No opinion
a)	A woman's place is in the home..........	11	15	22	24	27	1
b)	We should reduce pay differentials as much as possible....................	21	28	25	16	8	2
c)	Britain should keep its nuclear weapons even if other countries get rid of theirs.....................	14	16	15	26	27	1
d)	There are too many immigrants in Britain.............................	37	28	18	10	8	1
e)	Food additives should be banned.........	38	31	19	8	4	1
f)	I am very concerned about the level of pollution in Britain......	57	30	8	2	2	1
g)	You should do as little work as you can get away with....:...........	3	3	10	29	54	1
h)	Marriage is dead.........................	5	4	11	25	53	2
i)	It's time to reduce defence spending.....	20	27	25	16	11	1
j)	It is necessary to ban certain books.....	15	21	21	21	22	1
k)	Limits should be set for industrial growth.................................	9	23	32	21	12	2
l)	Conservation groups should be supported..	41	35	16	4	3	2
m)	The level of violence in British society is on the increase.............	56	34	5	3	2	1
n)	Trade unions are essential to protect workers' interests....................	24	34	21	14	7	1
o)	It is right to provide full financial support to the unemployed	22	35	20	16	5	1
p)	Children don't learn anything at at school anymore......................	7	15	17	33	26	1
q)	It's OK to pay workmen in cash to avoid having to pay VAT................	9	17	26	24	23	1
r)	In general, politicians are good people	4	31	40	16	7	1
s)	Britain needs a Bill of Rights to protect the liberty of the individual.............................	24	36	30	6	2	1
t)	The Common Market is a good thing for Britain.............................	11	33	28	17	11	1
u)	Football spectators should have to have identity cards....................	33	24	18	11	14	1

Base: All 1989 (1453)
nb Figures in brackets
= Base All 1983 (1030)

	Strongly agree %	Tend to agree %	Neither agree nor dis- agree %	Tend to disagree %	Strongly dis- agree %	No opinion
v) Japanese imports should be limited	27	35	24	9	3	1
w) Unemployment benefit should be reduced	5	10	23	33	28	2
x) The building of nuclear power stations has been a good thing for Britain	8	21	31	22	16	2
y) The troops should be withdrawn from Northern Ireland immediately	27	20	20	17	13	2
z) The police do their job well	26	44	13	11	3	2
aa) The Soviet Union remains a formidable threat to Britain's security	12	25	28	24	9	2
bb) Britain has lost its role in the world	16	34	21	21	6	2
cc) Europe needs nuclear weapons to defend itself	13	29	24	21	12	2
dd) Smoking in public places should be banned	37	24	15	12	8	1
ee) British Telecom should never have been privatised in the first place	26	17	35	14	8	1
ff) The government should ensure that all new cars only run on lead-free petrol	50	31	12	3	2	1
gg) The level of tax paid by wealthy people should be increased	41	26	16	10	5	2
hh) You can have confidence in the legal system	10	32	27	22	8	2
ii) Homosexuals should be treated just like other people	23	30	22	13	11	2
jj) We're not doing enough to control pornography	28	33	26	8	4	2
kk) It's a good thing that some people become very wealthy	13	27	30	19	9	2
ll) What young people need is strict discipline and a will to work and fight for a family and country	(53)40	(29)32	(7)16	(6)7	(4)4	(2)1

Base: All 1989 (1458)
nb Figures in brackets
= Base All 1983: (1030)

		Strongly agree %	Tend to agree %	Neither agree nor disagree %	Tend to disagree %	Strongly disagree %	No opinion %
mm)	People's lives are controlled by by accidental happenings..............	(12) 12	(37) 33	(12) 30	(26) 16	(11) 6	(2) 1
nn)	I feel that I have little influence over the things that happen to me.........................	(15) 10	(29) 26	(9) 20	(30) 33	(16) 11	(*) 1
oo)	What this country needs most, more than laws and political programmes, is a few courageous, tireless, devoted leaders in whom the people can put their faith..................	(43) 26	(29) 30	(5) 25	(14) 11	(7) 6	(2) 1
pp)	The pace of life is too much for me these days....................	(12) 8	(13) 8	(6) 23	(34) 34	(30) 17	(*) 1
qq)	My life seems to have been full of new and challenging opportunities..	(20) 16	(26) 28	(10) 27	(29) 21	(14) 7	(*) 1

RESPONDENT: THANK YOU. PLEASE GIVE QUESTIONNAIRE BACK TO INTERVIEWER

INTERVIEWER NOW COMPLETE DEMOGRAPHIC QUESTIONS ON PAGES 1,2,3. THANK YOU

SOCIAL CLASS DEFINITIONS

A   Professionals such as doctors, surgeons, solicitors or dentists; chartered people like architects; fully qualified people with a large degree of responsibility such as senior editors, senior civil servants, town clerks, senior business executives and managers, and high ranking grades of the Services.

B   People with very responsible jobs such as university lecturers, matrons of hospitals, heads of local government departments; middle management in business; qualified scientists, bank managers and upper grades of the Services, Police Inspectors.

C1 All others doing non-manual jobs; nurses, technicians, pharmacists, salesmen, publicans, people in clerical positions and middle ranks of the Services, Police Sergeants.

C2 Skilled manual workers/craftsmen who have served apprenticeships; foremen, manual workers with special qualifications such as long distance lorry drivers, security officers and lower grades of Services/Police Constables.

D   Semi-skilled and unskilled manual workers, including labourers and mates of occupations in the C2 grade and people serving apprenticeships; machine minders, farm labourers, bus and railway conductors, laboratory assistants, postmen, waiter/waitress, door-to-door and van salesman.

E   Those on lowest levels of subsistence including pensioners, casual workers, and others with minimum levels of income.

Index